THE CATHOLIC UNIVERSITY OF AMERICA
CANON LAW STUDIES
No. 129

RESTITUTIO IN INTEGRUM

AN HISTORICAL SYNOPSIS AND COMMENTARY

A DISSERTATION

Submitted to the Faculty of Canon Law of the Catholic University of America in Partial Fulfillment of the Requirements for the Degree of

DOCTOR OF CANON LAW

BY

REV. THOMAS JOHN FEENEY, A.B., S.T.L., J.C.L.
Priest of the Diocese of Davenport

THE CATHOLIC UNIVERSITY OF AMERICA PRESS
WASHINGTON, D. C.
1941

NIHIL OBSTAT:

Ludovicus Motry, S.T.D., J.C.D.,
Censor Deputatus.
Washingtonii, D. C., die VI Iunii, 1941.

IMPRIMATUR:

✠ Henricus P. Rohlman, D.D.,
Episcopus Davenportensis.
Davenporte, die VIII Iunii, 1941.

PRINTED IN THE UNITED STATES OF AMERICA
BY THE WATKINS PRINTING CO., BALTIMORE

TO

HIS EXCELLENCY

MOST REV. HENRY PATRICK ROHLMAN, D.D., LL.D.

IN

REVERENCE AND GRATITUDE

TABLE OF CONTENTS

Introduction 1

PART ONE—HISTORICAL SYNOPSIS

Chapter I. Roman Law 5
  Article I. Conditions 7
  Article II. Causes 8
  Article III. Procedure 11
Chapter II. Early Canon Law 13
  Article I. Before the Ninth Century 13
  Article II. From the Ninth Century to the Decree of Gratian 16
  Article III. The Decree of Gratian 19
Chapter III. Restitutio in the Decretal Law 22
  Article I. Requisivit—the first Decretal on Restitutio in Integrum 22
  Article II. The Law of the Decretals 25
    A. Conditions for Obtaining 27
    B. The Subject of the Remedy 29
    C. The Object of the Remedy 30
    D. Time Limit 34
    E. Procedure 35
    F. Effects 37
Chapter IV. From the Decretals to the Code of Canon Law 39
  Article I. Religious Profession 39
  Article II. Marriage Cases 41
  Article III. The Practice of the Roman Curia 44
Historical Summary 48

PART TWO—CANONICAL COMMENTARY

Section A. The Remedy in General

Chapter V. Definition 49
Chapter VI. The Subject of the Remedy 54
  Article I. Minors 55
  Article II. Persons Assimilated to Minors 58

Article III. Adults 61
CHAPTER VII. THE OBJECT OF THE REMEDY............ 69
Article I. Extra-Judicial Matters.................... 70
Article II. Judicial Matters 75
CHAPTER VIII. THE REMEDY AT WORK................ 79
Article I. Time Limit 79
Article II. The Competent Judge 82
Article III. Restitutio Granted "Ex Officio".......... 85
Article IV. Procedure 87
Article V. Effects 90
SECTION B. THE REMEDY AGAINST THE SENTENCE 94
CHAPTER IX. CONDITIONS FOR USE AGAINST THE SENTENCE 94
Article I. Res Iudicata 95
Article II. Appeal and Plaint of Nullity............. 96
Article III. Limits of Canons 1687-1688............. 101
Article IV. The Manifest Injustice of the Res Iudicata. 104
A. False Documents 105
B. New Documents 107
C. The Fraud of the Other Party 109
D. The Neglect of a Prescript of Law 110
CHAPTER X. THE NEGLECT OF A PRESCRIPT OF LAW...... 111
Article I. Restrictive Interpretation 114
Article II. Extensive Interpretation 117
Article III. Appraisal of the Opinions 121
Article IV. Conclusion 129
CHAPTER XI. THE CONCESSION OF THE REMEDY.......... 131
Article I. The Competent Court 131
Article II. Procedure 135
Article III. Effects 137
Article IV. Two Corollaries
A. The Criminal Sentence..................... 140
B. Restoration to Appeal 143
CONCLUSIONS 146
BIBLIOGRAPHY 149
ABBREVIATIONS 156
BIOGRAPHICAL NOTE 157
ANALYLICAL INDEX 158

INTRODUCTION

"He will judge the world with equity," sang the psalmist about the Lord God.[1] In keeping with its divine foundation, the Church of Christ as lawgiver and judge has always found a place for equity—"justice tempered by the sweetness of mercy" —in its system of law. Equity has been described as "a superior justice, the corrector of the existing law, the creator of new law to be applied in the particular case." [2] The present codification of the Church's law recalls to the minds of judges the application of equity many times. One procedural tool begotten of equity in the Roman law and adopted into the law of the Church is *restitutio in integrum.*

Restitutio in integrum is considered in the Code of Canon Law in two connections: in canons 1687-1689 as a remedy granted primarily to minors and to those enjoying the rights of minors, but also under some conditions to adults, who have suffered damage from a valid but rescissible act or transaction; in canons 1905-1907 as a remedy against the judicial sentence. In both these instances the only definition of the remedy given is one from its effects, stated in canon 1689: the effect of *restitutio in integrum* is that all things concerned are returned to their original condition, that is, they are restored to the state in which they were before the damage occurred.[3]

Canonists usually add to this definition the fact that *restitutio in integrum* is granted by a competent judge and because of natural equity. According to Reiffenstuel's definition, *restitutio in integrum* is "an extraordinary remedy of the law by which one who has been gravely damaged may, because of natural equity, be restored by a competent judge to that juridical status in which he was before being damaged." [4]

[1] Ps. XCV, 13.

[2] Van Hove, *De Legibus Ecclesiasticis,* Commentarium Lovaniense in Codicem Iuris Canonici, I, Tom. II (Mechliniae-Romae: Dessain 1930), n. 281.

[3] "Restitutio in integrum id efficit ut omnia revocentur in pristinum, idest restituantur in statum quo erant ante laesionem. . ."—canon 1689.

[4] Reiffenstuel, *Ius Canonicum Universum* (6 vols., Romae, 1831-1834), I,

A careful analysis of this definition will be made in Chapter V to preface the commentary on the present law and to ascertain whether the concept remains the same. For the present it will suffice to note that *restitutio* is allowed by the legislator because of "natural equity." For this reason it is an "extraordinary remedy." The strict law provides for the guarding of rights by ordinary means— the essentials of procedure are required under the pain of nullity of a trial; an appeal is usually allowed against an unjust sentence; court actions are provided to rescind acts performed through force and fear. Equity, however, prompts the lawgiver to provide in a general way for those particular circumstances when all other remedies are out of the question. He does so with *restitutio in integrum.* It is granted to minors because they are known to be frequently the victims of their own inexperience; it is allowed to churches and monasteries because like minors they are subject to the care of their guardians and should not suffer from the folly of their administrators; it is allowed to adults in certain circumstances because they too can find themselves bereft of any ordinary means of overcoming the legal injustice oppressing them.

The phrase "by a competent judge" in the definition shows that *restitutio* is a judicial act. For this reason it is included in Book IV of the Code of Canon Law, while in the Decretals of Gregory IX it was found in Book I, which concerned the Judge.

The Church enjoys not only the right to make its own laws which are binding upon its members, but also the right to enforce its laws, to declare in an authoritative manner whether the actions of its subjects are in conformity with the law or not, to decide what the legitimate effects of compliance to the law or disregard for it will be. In short, it also enjoys judicial power. This is derived not only from the fact that the Church

tit. 41, n. 3; cf. Wernz, *Ius Decretalium,* Vol. V, *De Iudiciis Ecclesiasticis* (3. ed. Prati, 1914), p. 556; Coronata, *Institutiones Iuris Canonici,* Vol. III, *De Processibus* (Taurini: Marietti, 1933), n. 1215.

is a perfect society in which judicial power is inherent, but also from its divine founder Himself who bestowed judicial power on His apostles and their successors.[5]

To attain justice, in as far as it is humanly possible, in the exercise of its judicial power, the Church borrowed from the Roman law the remedy under discussion. It would be erroneous to conclude, of course, whenever a legal institution of the Church resembles one which preexisted in Roman law, that the ecclesiastical law borrowed from the civil. But in the case of *restitutio in integrum* it is universally admitted that this remedy was adopted from Roman procedure. It will be necessary then to look back to the Roman law not only for the origin of the remedy but also to some extent for its interpretation. The Code of Canon Law does not mention the Roman law as an aid for the interpretation of its canons. Nevertheless, in the case of legal institutions taken bodily from the Roman law, that law cannot be ignored in an attempt to understand and apply them properly.[6]

After a discussion of the remedy in Roman law the adoption and development of it will be traced in canon law down to the promulgation of the Code in 1918. Since the Code treats of *restitutio* in two different places in the fourth book, the second part of this dissertation, which comments on the present law, will be divided into two sections. In the first the general law on the remedy, canons 1687-1689, will be explained; in the second application will be made to its use against a particular act, the judicial sentence, in a commentary on the specific regulations set up by the Code in canons 1905-1907.

No English equivalent of the phrase *restitutio in integrum* has been universally accepted. Perhaps the translation which best demonstrates the meaning of the original term is "restoration

[5] Matth. XVIII, 15-18. Cf. Ottaviani, *Institutiones Iuris Publici Ecclesiastici* (2. ed., 2 vols., Romae: Typis Polyglottis Vaticanis, 1935), I, n. 145.

[6] Cf. Coronata, *Ius Publicum Ecclesiasticum* (2. ed., Taurini: Marietti, 1934) n. 195; Van Hove, *Prolegomena,* Commentarium Lovaniense in Codicem Iuris Canonici, I, Tom. I (Mechliniae-Romae: Dessain, 1928), n. 96.

to previous condition." [7] This phrase is too lengthy to be used with ease in English. Other writers have attempted to use "reinstatement," but because it has the restricted connotation of persons being reinstated in office, in membership, or the like, it does not suit the more general concept of this remedy. Even those authors who use "reinstatement" take refuge in supplying the Latin term parenthetically.[8] To retain, therefore, the full and precise Roman and canon law concept of this remedy, the Latin form, *restitutio in integrum,* has been used.

[7] Used frequently by Sherman, *Roman Law in the Modern World* (3. ed., 3 vols., New York: Baker, Voorhis & Co., 1937), II, 112, *et passim.*

[8] Cf. Roby, *Roman Private Law* (2 vols., Cambridge, 1902), II, 259; Smith, *Elements of Ecclesiastical Law,* II, *Ecclesiastical Trials* (New York, 1882), 358.

PART I
Historical Synopsis

CHAPTER I
ROMAN LAW

Restitutio in integrum was created by the Roman praetor as a remedy to revoke or to treat as non-existing some act which prejudiced the legal position of a person.

The praetorship dates from one of the Licinian Rogations of 367 B.C., which created the office as an assistant to the consul, transferring to the praetor the control over litigation.[1] The praetor held office for one year in which, like the consul, he was invested with the judicial powers of the ancient kings. He exercised both *iurisdictio* and *imperium*. With his jurisdiction he administered the civil law by presiding over the preliminary stages of litigation; with his *imperium* he could give commands and enforce them by fines or imprisonment, summon parties before him and conduct in person an investigation of a case. He was not, however, a judge in the modern sense. Before the third century of the Christian era the Roman trial was conducted in two stages; one, called *in iure,* was held before the praetor who, having heard the parties, formulated the issue at stake; the other, the actual trial as to the merits of the case, and called *in iudicio,* was held before a judge who was chosen as an arbiter for the case.

Among the powers of the praetor was the granting of remedies against the law, giving relief where the strict law bound too rigorously. Most notable among the praetorian remedies was *restitutio in integrum.* Here the praetor exercised his *imperium* to restore a person who had been damaged in his proprty or his

[1] Livy, 6, 42.

rights to the status he held before the damaging act occurred.

It is impossible to determine with any exactness when the praetor began to use this remedy. That it was in use at the time of Cicero is certain from the allusions he made to it, as in his second oration for Verres.[2] Romanists are not in accord in setting any more exact date for its origin; neither are they in agreement as to which cause for restoration the praetor first recognized: whether he first granted the *restitutio minorum* or some *restitutio* for adults because of absence, or fear, or fraud; likewise whether *restitutio* was the primitive remedy in the case of force, fear, fraud, and error, which was superseded in part by ordinary actions, or whether *restitutio* was a later remedy added to these to supply for their defects is disputed. For the purpose of this dissertation which is concerned with the Roman law only as a basis of the canon law these purely historical questions are of slight import.[3] It is sufficient to note that *restitutio in integrum* was in use by the time of Cicero (+ 43 B. C.) and was well developed by the beginning of the Christian era.

This remedy underwent some changes, however, between the date of its origin and the Justinian compilations. The greatest change is noted in the very nature of the remedy from the way in which the sources refer to it: at first it is an *auxilium extraordinarium,* over which the praetor had arbitrary control; later it is referred to as *beneficium,* a legal remedy granted in definite circumstances.[4]

It is not difficult to understand how such a development would

[2] *In Verr.* 2, 2, 26, 63; cf. also *Pro Flacco,* 31 76—*M. Tulii Ciceronis Orationes* (ed. Peterson, Oxonii, 1916) and *Ciceronis pro Flacco* (ed. Clark, Oxonii, n. d.). Cf. Costa, *Profilo Storico del Processo Civile Romano* (Roma, 1918), p. 85; Jolowicz, *An Historical Introduction to the Study of Roman Law* (Cambridge: University Press, 1932), p. 97; 230, note 2.

[3] For some discussion and a bibliography on these questions cf. Gallet, "Essai sur le Senatus-Consulte 'de Asclepiade Sociisque'," *Revue Historique de Droit Français et Etranger,* XVI (1937), 407-425; likewise Jolowicz, *op. cit.,* p. 230 note 2.

[4] Carelli gives many citations of both forms—"Sul 'beneficium restitutionis'," *Studia et Documenta Historiae et Iuris,* IV (1938), 5 ff.

come about. In the beginning when the praetor began to grant *restitutio in integrum,* he did so in the individual case whenever he felt that equity demanded it; then he listed in his edict the cases and conditions under which he would grant the remedy. His successors changed the edict but little; and the jurisconsults tended to crystalize the clauses of the edict by their commentaries. A precedent was thus set up with the result that the injured party came to have a subjective right to *restitutio* rather than a mere hope of it from the praetor.[5] In spite of this change the law on the remedy remained fairly constant throughout the centuries. From the edict and the writings of the jurisconsults that have been preserved, together with the enactments of the emperors, the conditions which the praetor required for *restitutio in integrum* as well as the typical cases and the procedure he used in considering them can be pieced together.

Article I. Conditions

A. *Damage* Primary among the conditions for *restitutio* was that the party seeking the remedy must have suffered damage or injury—that he was in a worse state than he had been and wished now to be restored to his original condition.[6] This damage had to be of considerable size,[7] but the measure of it was left to the discretion of the praetor. This damage was understood as either loss of something possessed or the cessation of profit from a thing.[8] Its existence, moreover, had to be proven to the praetor,

B. *No other remedy.* Another condition was that there be no other remedy at hand to repair the loss. For *restitutio in*

[5] Just when this change was accomplished is not clear; Carelli (*op. cit.,* p. 65) musters a great mass of interpolated texts to prove that it took place in the post-classical period.

[6] C. (4, 1) 1; 4.

[7] D. (4, 4) 9, pr.; (4, 1) 4. This latter text gave rise to the frequently misunderstood axiom: *De minimis non curat praetor*; it is termed simply *falso adagio* by Bonfante—*Storia del Diritto Romano* (3. ed., 2 vols., Milano: Societa Editrice Libraria, 1923), I, 459, note 1.

[8] D. (4, 6) 27.

integrum was an extraordinary remedy, and, as Ulpian pointed out, he who has an ordinary remedy should not be given an extraordinary one.[9] Therefore if a transaction were null by law, this remedy would not be given.[10]

In some cases *restitutio* was ruled out by the law. For instance, the gift of liberty to a slave—*manumissio*—was considered so irrevocable that neither a minor [11] nor the republic itself could be restored to ownership.[12] Neither could this remedy be used to begin a criminal action which had been neglected within the period allowed for bringing suit.[13] Nor would it be granted to anyone for the reparation of damage suffered from his own wrongdoing.[14]

C. *Time.* Since the praetor's term of office continued but one year, he did not promise any remedy over a longer period. During the classical period, therefore, application for *restitutio* had to be made within a year from the time of the damage, the time not running, however, if the person were impeded from action.[15] In the case of a minor, the year began upon his reaching his majority. Constantine set up different time limits for this remedy in various regions,[16] but Justinian swept away these distinctions and set up a four year period—*quadriennium continuum*—that is, four calendar years which began to run from the time of majority or from the time the damage occurred unless something impeded the person from seeking the remedy.[17]

Article II. Causes

Granted that someone had suffered damage, the praetor required also a just cause for *restitutio in integrum.* Chief among

[9] D. (4, 4) 16, pr., though interpolated, is to be attributed to Ulpian in substance; cf. Carelli, *op. cit.*, p. 31.

[10] D. (4, 4) 16, pr., 3.

[11] D. (4, 4) 9, 6.

[12] D. (49, 1) 9.

[13] D. 4, 4) 37, pr.

[14] D. (4, 4) 9, 2.

[15] "*annus utilis*"—C. (2, 52) 7; cf. D. (4, 4) 19.

[16] C. Th. (2, 16) 2.

[17] C. (2, 52) 7.

those listed in the sources were: minority, absence, force and fear, and error.

A. *Minority.* When dealing with a youth under twenty-five years of age, the praetor would grant this remedy if the inexperience of the minor had allowed his property or his position to be damaged. The damage had to be due to the fraud of another person or to the minor's own inexperience—*inconsulta facilitas*—and not to chance or to an accident.[18] The transactions in which this remedy was open to the minor were many. The edict of the praetor read *Quod cum minore. . .gestum esse dicetur* to protect all phases of the minor's civic life.[19] From the many types of transaction listed in the sources it is safe to conclude that the praetor would grant this remedy to a minor in any case in which his edict or the law had not expressly excluded it. For example, a minor would not be restored to his previous condition if he had lied about his age, pretending to be of full age so that the other party would deal with him;[20] or, in imperial times, if he had received a rescript from the emperor—*venia aetatis*—allowing him to act as one of full age;[21] or if, after reaching his majority, he had ratified the transaction.[22] The fact, however, that he had been aided by his tutor in the deal would not necessarily exclude him from the remedy.[23]

B. *Absence.* Absence was the chief ground on which a person over twenty-five years of age could invoke the use of *restitutio*.[24] The remedy could be granted either in favor of or against the one who was absent. In the first case, if a person suffered the loss of a thing, or a right, or was unable to act within the time prescribed by law because of his absence, he could ask for this remedy upon his return. The absence could be due to fear

[18] D. (4, 4) 44; 11, 4.
[19] D. (4, 4) 1, 1.
[20] C. (2, 42) 2.
[21] C. (2, 44) 1.
[22] C. (2, 45) 2.
[23] D. (4, 4) 29, pr.
[24] D. (4, 1) 8.

of death or of bodily torture.[25] It could be for public service—*rei publicae causa*—such as a legation to the emperor,[26] or military service, even right in the city of Rome;[27] magistrates in Rome, however, were not considered absent for public service.[28] The absence again could be caused by imprisonment so that one could physically appear in court, but not without shame.[29]

But the praetor at his discretion could interpret absence even more broadly. *Item si qua alia mihi iusta causa esse videbitur, in integrum restituam,* he promised.[30] This general clause, as it was termed even in the sources, meant that whenever a person omitted the defense of his rights or property by necessity rather than voluntarily he would be helped by the praetor. The person must have exercised due diligence to avoid the loss or damage; the remedy was to aid not the negligent but those impeded by necessity. If a person had appointed a procurator who might have defended him, he would not receive the benefit of this remedy.[31]

Restitutio in integrum against an absentee, on the other hand, was granted to one who suffered loss by not being able to bring suit against an absent party who could thus complete usucapion or gain freedom from a servitude or from an action.[32]

C. *Fear and force.* If a person were damaged because he was forced into a transaction by threats of violence, he could be restored to his previous condition.[33] But there were ordinary remedies, e. g., an *actio quod metus causa* and an exception, for such cases; perhaps the rule cited above from Ulpian that an extraordinary remedy is not to be given when an ordinary one is available did not hold here so that a person who had been

[25] D. (4, 6) 3.
[26] C. (2, 53) 1.
[27] D. (4, 6) 7.
[28] D. (4, 6) 5, 1; 6.
[29] D. (4, 6) 9; 10; 1, 1.
[30] D. (4, 6) 1, 1.
[31] D. (4, 6) 39.
[32] D. (4, 6) 1, pr.
[33] D. (4, 2) 1.

intimidated had his choice of remedies.[34] If the wrongdoer had become insolvent, *restitutio in integrum* was a better remedy as it rescinded the forced alienation and separated the property of the one intimidated from the assets over which the other creditors had a claim.

Other causes for *restitutio* were deception (*dolus*),[35] and error[36] of which slight traces are found in the sources.

Article III. Procedure

The procedure involved in granting a *restitutio in integrum* underwent a change together with the whole of Roman procedure. During the ascendancy of the *ordo indiciorum privatorum* the praetor or the provincial governor[37] received the petition for the remedy and held an investigation; this was not a trial but a simple examination to determine whether an equitable cause and sufficient damage required his time and diligence and whether there were not some ordinary remedy available. Satisfied on these points, the praetor would issue a decree conceding the remedy.[38] This resembled the *in iure* proceedings of a trial and was carried out by the praetor himself. If the case involved the loss of an action or of a property right, an *actio rescissoria* followed in which by a fiction it was held that the damaging fact never occurred; this *actio,* at least during the formulary period, was usually committed to a judge.[39]

With the rise of the *cognitio extraordinaria* the division of a Roman trial into two parts gradually disappeared. The whole trial took place before a judge who represented the state. The investigation which was held before the granting of this remedy thus came to resemble any other process: a petition (libellus) was

[34] Cf. Buckland, *A Text Book of Roman Law from Augustus to Justinian* (2. ed., Cambridge: University Press, 1932), p. 593.

[35] D. (4, 1) 7, 1.

[36] D. (4, 1) 2.

[37] C. (2, 53) 2; D. (4, 4) 42.

[38] Carelli gives an outline of the early procedure in granting this remedy—*op. cit.*, p. 7.

[39] Cf. Buckland, *op. cit.*, p. 723.

presented; the other party was summoned, the issue joined, proofs offered, and finally a judgment passed which either granted or refused the remedy.[40]

The changes in Roman procedure had a further effect on *restitutio in integrum* against the decision rendered by a judge. In the period of the *ordo iudiciorum privatorum,* when an appointed arbiter acted as judge, there was no appeal possible. Yet the magistrate could grant this extraordinary remedy even against his own decision or that of his predecessor.[41] Such a *restitutio* struck not at the decision of the judge but at the *litis contestatio* and the decision necessarily fell with it. After a new *litis contestatio* the action would be retried. Such a proceeding could be invoked only in harmony with the general conditions for this remedy and for a just cause. The failure to defend oneself could constitute such a cause.

In the *cognitio extraordinaria,* however, the *litis contestatio* lost its prime importance as a contractual agreement which transformed the rights of the parties on the matter in dispute. Only the decision of the judge came to have that effect.[42] Thus *restitutio in integrum* had to strike not at the *litis contestatio* but at the sentence of the judge. At the same time the institution of appeals became common. The distinction between the two remedies was this: An appeal was a remedy against the injustice of the sentence, while *restitutio* was to be used in case of error on the part of the judge or of deception on the part of the opposing party.[43] In this sense *restitutio in integrum* became a remedy quite similar to the appeal and as such was habitually used by Justinian.[44]

[40] For a comparison in general of the procedure of the two periods, cf. Wenger, *Institutes of the Roman Law of Civil Procedure,* translated by Fisk (New York: Veritas Press, 1940), § 25, pp. 255-268.

[41] D. (4, 4) 17; 42; 16, 5.

[42] Cf. Wenger, *op. cit.,* § 28, p. 290.

[43] Cf. D. (4, 4) 17.

[44] Cf. Biondi, *Appunti intorno alla Sentenza nel Processo Civile Romano* (Pavia: Successori Fratelli Fusi, 1929), pp. 97-99.

Chapter II

EARLY CANON LAW

Article I. Before The Ninth Century

Since *restitutio in integrum* was a mature legal institution of the Romans before the birth of Christ, the question to be answered in an attempt to trace the history of it in canon law is not when and where it originated, but when and how it was introduced into the canonical procedure. The trials held in the early Christian communities were simple affairs. The principles governing them were drawn chiefly from the Sacred Scriptures and from the natural law.[1]

When the persecutions ceased under Constantine (313), the Church was able to live in the open so that the ecclesiastical court experienced a notable growth. Moreover, Constantine in two constitutions, one in 318 [2] and another to Ablabius in 333, recognized the jurisdiction of the ecclesiastical courts.[3] The nature of the jurisdiction which the *audientia episcopalis* enjoyed as a result of these and other imperial enactments [4] is not beyond dispute. Whether in the eyes of the civil authority the Bishops tried civil cases merely as arbiters [5] or as ordinary judges [6] cannot be settled here.

[1] Cf. Wernz-Vidal, *Ius Canonicum,* Vol. VI, *De Processibus* (Romae: Universitas Gregoriana, 1927), n. 2; cf. *Didascalia,* II, cc. 45 ff., ed. Funk, *Didascalia et Constitutiones Apostolorum* (2 vols., Paderbornae, 1905), I, 138-148.

[2] C. Th. (1, 27) 1. Its authenticity is generally admitted; cf. Dareste, *Revue Historique de Droit Français et Etranger,* 4. série, V. (1926), 703.

[3] *Const. Sirmondiana I—Theodosiani Libri XVI,* ed. Mommsen-Meyer (3 vols., Berolini, 1905), I, 907 f. The authenticity of this constitution, though strongly attacked by some, is now quite generally recognized; cf. Wenger, *Institutes,* § 26, p. 342, note 11; Vismara, *Episcopalis Audientia.* Pubblicazioni della U. Cattolica del Sacro Cuore, 2. serie, Scienze Giuridiche, n. LIV (Milano: Vita e Pensiero, 1937), p. 21.

[4] Cf. C. Th. (1, 27) 2, i. e. C. (1, 4) 8; C. Th. (16, 2) 1; 23.

[5] Thus, de Francisci, *Per la storia dell' Audientia Episcopalis fino alla Nov. XXXV (XXXIV) di Valentiniano* (Roma, 1915), p. 9; Onory,

But in his constitution of 333 Constantine decreed that the decision of a bishop was to be preserved intact without any distinction as to the age of the parties to the trial; that whether they be minors or adults the judgment of the bishop should be executed.[7] Did Constantine intend by this to eliminate *restitutio in integrum* against the sentence of a bishop? *Restitutio* was the remedy primarily of minors, and in the matter of appeals minors and adults were on the same footing. It would seem that the intention of this constitution was to rule out the concession of *restitutio* in favor of minors by a civil magistrate against a bishop's judgment.[8]

Even if this supposition be true, it merely demonstrates that the emperor made the sentence rendered in the *audientia episcopalis* enforceable to a very high degree. It gives no hint as to whether *restitutio in integrum* was used in the episcopal courts. Would a bishop, for example,, rescind the contract of a minor by *restitutio?* Other imperial sources which legislated concerning the episcopal court do not answer this question. And the references of the ecclesiastical writers in the early centuries to *restitutio* are very meager.

Pope Leo the Great (+ 461), for example, speaks of *restitutio in integrum* in a letter to the Emperor Leo Augustus (457-474), recommending that this remedy should not be used in favor of Timothy, Bishop of Alexandria, whom the emperor had deposed. Because of his great crimes, Pope Leo did not want him

Vescovi e Citta (*Sec. IV-VI*), Biblioteca della Rivista di Storia del Diritto Italiano, n. 8 (Bologna: Zanichelli, 1933), p. 56.

6 Thus, Vismara, *Episcopalis Audientia,* pp. 16-17.

7 ". . . sententias episcoporum, quolibet genere latas, sine aliqua aetatis discretione inviolatas semper incorruptas servari . . . Sive itaque inter minores sive inter majores ab episcopis fuerit iudicatum . . . ad executionem volumus pertinere"—*Const. Sirmondiana I.*

8 Whether this constitution, granted its authenticity, intended to exclude *restitutio* is disputed. Cf. Busek, "Episcopalis Audientia, eine Frieden-und Schiedsgerichtsbarkeit," *Zeitschrift der Savigny-Stiftung für Rechtsgeschichte,* LIX (1939), Kan. Abt. XXVIII, 457, note 1; Dareste, *Revue Historique de Droit Français et Etranger,* 4. série, V (1926), 705.

restored to his see.[9] Such a *restitutio in integrum* would be similar to that which the Emperor Caracalla (211-217) granted to a man who had been deported because of a crime.[10] It was an act rather of mercy than of justice and would not fall under the concept of the praetorian remedy.

St. Jerome (+ 420) has a very apt but non-juridical allusion to this remedy when he compares the effects of penance to those of *restitutio*.[11] It is mentioned also by St. Isidore of Seville (+ 636). In his collection of etymologies he gives a definition of the remedy: "Integri restitutio est causae vel rei reparatio." [12] He did not amplify his definition in any way.

Such references, though they be multiplied through a diligent search of non-legal sources, point rather to a familiarity with Roman law on the part of the Christian writers than to the use of this remedy in canonical trials. Only with the collections of the ninth century do references to this remedy become at all frequent. Since there are such meager traces of the institution of *restitutio in integrum* in ecclesiastical writers prior to that time, it should be noted that other means were provided to give the protection which this remedy later gave when it became incorporated into canon law.

In Roman law, minors, absentees, and the victims of force, fear, and fraud were helped by *restitutio*. In the early sources of canon law, however, there is no specific remedy to aid a youth who has been the loser in a transaction because of his own inexperience; this may well have been left to the secular court. In the case of absence, though the absentee was not

[9] ". . . et in integrum valeret qualibet conditione restitui, nequaquam tamen . . ."—Ep. 169, dated June 17, 460—*MPL,* LIV, 1212; CSEL, XXXV, part I, 117-118.

[10] C. (9, 51) 1.

[11] *Commentarium in Ecclesiasten,* cap. 1— *MPL,* XXIII, 1022; cf. Violardo, *Il Pensiero Giuridico di San Girolamo,* Pubblicazioni della U. Cattolica del Sacro Cuore, 2. serie, Scienze Giuridiche, n. LV (Milano: Vita e Pensiero, 1937), p. 244.

[12] Lib. V, cap. 25, *de rebus,* n. 36— *Isidori Hispalensis Episcopi Etymologiarum sive Originum Libri XX,* ed. W. M. Lindsay (Oxonii, 1911); *MPL,* LXXXII, 209.

helped in every respect by the ecclesiastical court, the enactments of some of the councils prohibited the trial of one who was not present; the Council of Chalcedon (451) proclaimed the nullity of any sentence passed against an absent person.[13] Likewise a sentence pronounced under compulsion of fear was declared invalid by the VI Roman Synod, held under the Pope Symmachus in 504: "An unjust trial and the unjust decision rendered by the judges with fear of or at the order of the king is invalid." [14]

Article II. From The Ninth Century To The Decree of Gratian

Since the first collections of canon law in the West were almost exclusively composed of the legislation of the councils, nothing on *restitutio in integrum* appears in them because the councils, general or particular, did not consider this remedy for ecclesiastical processes. But the authors of the collections from the beginning of the ninth century up to Gratian began to add complete sections of Roman law to the canonical legislation.[15]

Among the first of these was Benedict the Levite, whose *Capitularia* (*circa* 850) purported to be a continuation of the authentic collection of Frankish law made earlier in the century by Ansegisus.[16] Among the alleged canonical documents added by Benedict were many texts from Roman law; these borrowings were not all confined to dispositions of ecclesiastical matters but were of general import. Such was his section *De integra*

[13] ". . . Quae adversus absentem facta sunt, vacuentur"—Actio X, c. 6—Harduin, *Acta Conciliorum et Epistolae Decretales ac Constitutiones Summorum Pontificum* (12 vols., Paris, 1714-1715), II, 507; cf. also IV Council of Carthage (398), can. 30—Harduin, I, 981.

[14] "Iniustum enim iudicium, et defensio iniusta, regio metu vel iussu a iudicibus ordinata, non valet"—Harduin, II, 993.

[15] Cf. Van Hove, *Prolegomena,* n. 94.

[16] The identity of Benedict is uncertain. This work probably originated near Le Mans, France, between 847 and 857. Cf. Fournier-Le Bras, *Histoirè des Collections Canoniques en Occident depuis les fausses décrétales jusq'au decret de Gratien* (2 vols., Paris: Recueil Sirey, 1931-1932), 196 ff.

restitutione,[17] which was taken bodily, not from the Justinian compilations, but from the *Breviary of Alaric.* This body of law, more properly called the *Lex Romana Visigothorum,* was promulgated by Alaric II in 506 for the use of the Roman citizens in Visigothic Spain, though it came to enjoy much wider recognition..[18] It was composed chiefly of abbreviations of the "Opinions of Paulus," the Theodosian Code, and the Institutes of Gaius, with an *interpretatio* added throughout. The section which Benedict adopted on *restitutio* is from the interpretation added to the "Opinions of Paulus."[19] It confused the restoration of a thing taken by force or stealth [20] with *restitutio in integrum* as made by the praetor. It likewise permitted a free-born person who had sold himself into slavery to regain his ingenuitas through this remedy. This was explicitly denied in Roman law.[21]

Two other collections contemporary with that of Benedict and also convicted of forgeries—the *Capitularies of Angilram* and the *Pseudo-Isidorian Decretals*—contain nothing on *restitutio in integrum.* But together these three collections include many forged texts to handle in one way or another the same problems for which this remedy would provide.[22] To assert the nullity of acts performed through fear, a passage from the Roman

[17] Lib. VII, c. 288—Mansi, *Sacrorum Conciliorum Nova et Amplissima Collectio* (53 vols., Paris- Arnhem-Leipzig, 1901-1927), XVII-B, 1089.

[18] Haenel, *Lex Romana Visigothorum* (Leipzig, 1849), p. VI; Laurin, *Introductio in Corpus Iuris Canonici* (Friburgi Brisgoviae et Vindobonae, 1889), p. 266.

[19] *Pauli Sententiarum,* lib. I, tit. 7— Haenel, *Lex Romana Visigothorum,* pp. 344-345.

[20] "id quod alicui sublatum est . . . de his quae iniuste ablata sunt . . . is qui rem indebite abstulisse convincitur . . ."—Benedict, lib. VII, cc. 288-289.

[21] D. (4, 4) 9, 4. Cf. Buckland, *The Roman Law of Slavery* (Cambridge, 1908), p. 428.

[22] It is not beyond dispute which of the three collections is to be considered the parent in the case of documents appearing in two or in all three; the Pseudo-Isidorian is usually considered the last. Though some of the documents mentioned here by way of example are to be found in all three collections, citations will be given only with reference to the Pseudo-Isidore.

Synod in 504 was attributed to Pope Callixtus (+ 227),[23] and Pope Alexander (+ c. 132) was credited with a statement from the Breviary of Alaric that a judicial confession extorted by fear was null.[24] And to emphasize the fact that a trial held during the absence of the accused was not only forbidden but also null, decretals were assigned to Popes Eleutherius (+ c. 193),[25] Cornelius (+ 255),[26] and Felix I (+ 275) among others.[27]

At about the same time with the false decretals there appeared in Italy a collection of Roman law intended for the clergy, the *Lex Romana Canonice Compta* (c. 850), which included law that was not solely on ecclesiastical subjects. Among the secular matters treated are four paragraphs on *restitutio in integrum* granted to minors and to the victims of force and fear.[28] Very shortly thereafter the as yet unpublished *Collectio Anselmo Dedicata* (c. 882) incorporated these four paragraphs on the remedy.[29]

More important is the treatment of *restitutio* by Ives of Chartres (+ 1116) in his *Decretum*, which appeared between 1090 and 1095. He devoted a short chapter to each of the grounds for the remedy—fear, absence, and minority. He placed them in the part of his work entitled "Concerning the duties of the laity and their causes." [30] Because of their position under this heading, perhaps Ives did not intend that this remedy should be used in the ecclesiastical courts. Though the first chapters of this part of his *Decretum* were taken from the work of

[23] Hinschius, *Decretales Pseudo-Isodorianae et Capitula Angilramni* (Lipsiae, 1863), c. 6, p. 137.

[24] Hinschius, *op.* cit., c. 7, p. 97.

[25] Hinschius, op. cit., c. 5, p. 126, taken from the IV Council of Carthage.

[26] Taken from the Council of Chalcedon, *Actio X*—Hinschius, *op. cit.*, c. 6, p. 174.

[27] Taken from the Breviary of Alaric—Hinschius, *op. cit.*, c. 11, p. 202.

[28] Mor, *Lex Romana Canonice Compta, Testo di leggi romano-canoniche del sec. IX* (Pavia: Tipografia Cooperativa, 1927), nn. 285, 306-308.

[29] In Book VII. Mor collates the two collections—*op. cit.*, p. 29 ff.

[30] Pars XVI, cc. 168, 169, and 205—*MPL*, CLXI, 937, 944.

Burchard of Worms (+ 1025), the latter sections were borrowed from Roman law.[31] Ives cited the Roman law directly from the Digest rather than from any intermediate source.

Research outside the canonical collections of this period reveals that Gregory VII used the phrase *in integrum restituere* or its equivalent several times in his letters. In one letter [32] it is clearly a case of restoration of one who has been despoiled, an application of the Psudo-Isidorian principle, "Spoliatus ante omnia est restituendus." [33] In another letter, it is apparently used to refer to the restoration of what has been taken by force. But a third case seems to fit into the mold of the praetorian remedy of *restitutio.* When two abbeys disputed the possession of the church of St. Mary's of Soulac, Gregory wrote to the Bishop of Oloron in Gascony to reinstate the Abbey of the Holy Cross in Bordeaux in possession and then to act as one of the judges in the trial concerning the ownership.[34]

Article III. The Decree of Gratian.

Gratian, whose *Concordia Discordantium Canonum* (c. 1140) became the most widely-known canoncial collection prior to the Decretals of Gregory IX, made short shrift of *restitutio in integrum.* The references to it in his *Decretum,* as it is now known, are few and for the greater part in his own *dicta,* that is, they are not in the laws he collected but in his comments upon the laws; the *dicta* are but the opinion of a canonist and not law.

It is difficult to say why Gratian did not give more importance to the remedy under discussion. In other cases he did not

[31] Cf. Fournier, *Les Collections Attribueés a Yves de Chartres* (Paris, 1897), p. 48.

[32] Ep. IX, 33—*Das Register Gregors VII,* ed. Erich Casper—*MGH, Epistolae Selectae* (2 vols., Berolini: apud Weidmannos, 1920-1923), II, 620.

[33] Cf. Van Hove, *Prolegomena,* n. 166; Crump and Jacob, *The Legacy of the Middle Ages* (Oxford: Clarendon Press, 1932), p. 350, in the chapter on "Canon Law" by Gabriel Le Bras.

[34] *Ep.* VI, 24, March 8, 1079—*MGH, Epistolae Selectae,* I, 436.

refuse to invoke the civil law.[35] And the collection of Ives of Chartres and that which was known as the *Anselmo Dedicata*, which treated of this institution, were among his sources.[36] Perhaps it was because of the insignificance of *restitutio in integrum* in the canon law of the preceding centuries; perhaps he felt that such a remedy were best left to the secular court. At all events, on the real praetorian remedy he has nothing. Twice in the course of the third question of Cause III he mentions *restitutio in integrum* in his *dicta*. The first time it is in connection with the difficulty of a text attributed to Pope Gelasius, "Though we can save souls through penance, we cannot wipe out infamy." [37] Gratian's solution is that the Pope spoke of infamy imposed by a civil judge so that "just as the examination and the punishing, so too the restoration pertains to the civil judge."

At the end of the question he explains this civil *in integrum restitutio*. Abolition of a penalty does not remove infamy, but *in integrum restitutio* does. In proof of this he quotes from a constitution of the Emperor Caracalla (211-217), who granted such a restoration to a man who had been deported because of crime, saying, "Restituo te in integrum provinciae tuae." And in order that the man would know the import of this favor, the emperor explained that it was a restoration "to honors, and to your own order, and to all else." [38] Rufinus (+ c. 1190), an early glossator of Gratian's work, writing on this text in his *Summa Decreti* about 1159, explained that infamy sometimes could not be remitted; and when it could be remitted, if the crime were such a great one as homicide or adultery, it was only through *restitutio in integrum*.[39] Such a restoration, how-

[35] Cf. Laurin, *Introductio*, p. 17; also Friedberg in the introduction to his edition of Gratian—*Corpus Iuris Canonici*, editio Lipsiensis II (2 vols., Lipsiae, 1879-1881), I, p. LIV.

[36] Laurin, *Introductio*, p. 19.

[37] Friedberg in his notes says the text is rather from the pseudo-Isidorian decretal of Callixtus—*Corpus Iuris Canonici*, I, 453, note 66.

[38] C. (9, 51) 1.

[39] ". . . tunc solum remittitur, quando eis restitutio prioris status in integrum reparatur; ut laico quando sufficienter peracta penitentia ex toto

ever, as Durantis (+ 1296) points out later, is not *restitutio in integrum* in the strict sense, for this restoration was given *ex misericordia,* while the praetorian remedy was granted *ex iustitia.*[40]

The phrase *in integrum restituantur* appears in a decretal attributed to Pope Julius I (341-352) and was taken by Gratian from the false decretals. Again this reference is not to the remedy under discussion but to the restoration of the despoiled, with which many of the neighboring texts of the second question of Cause II are concerned.[41]

Up to the time of Gratian, then, it is evident that *restitutio in integrum* was not a common remedy in the ecclesiastical court. The term had been loosely used to denote an act of mercy by Pope or Prince (as in the letter of Leo I and in Gratian's *dicta*) or to denote the restitution of ill-gotten goods (as in Benedict the Levite and Gregory VII). In those collections in which the remedy was explained as applied by the Roman praetor, it is either in a non-canonical collection like the *Lex Romana Canonice Compta,* or in a section of a canonical collection which applied perhaps solely to the laity, as in the *Decretum* of Ives of Chartres.

ecclesiasticae communioni redditur, ut clerico quando in suum officium restituitur"—*Die Summa Decretorum des Magister Rufinus,* ed. H. Singer (Paderborn, 1902), p. 246.

[40] *Speculum Iuris Guglielmi Durandi* (3 vols., Venetiis, 1577), lib. II, partic. III, *h. t.,* n. 34.

[41] C. 5, C. II, q. 2. Gratian or some intermediate source must have changed the text to read *in integrum restituantur*; Hinschius (*op. cit.,* p. 473) says its source is the III Synod at Rome (more properly the fourth, or Romana Palmaris); Friedberg (*Corpus Iuris Canonici,* I, 451) says it is derived from the *Apologia* of Ennodius for that synod (cf. Mansi, VIII, 271 ff.). But neither the synod nor the *Apologia* nor even the text of Pseudo-Isidore have this particular phrase. Likewise Benedict the Levite (VII, 116—Mansi, XVII-B, 1048) and Burchard of Worms (I, 144—*MPL,* CXL, 591) and Ives of Chartres (*Decretum*—*MPL,* CLXI, 403; *Pannormia*—*MPL* CLXI, 1193) reproduce the false decretal of Julius but without the phrase *in integrum restituantur.* Perhaps Gratian himself altered the text to make the restoration of the despoiled approximate the civil restoration of which he speaks in his *dicta* of C. III, q. 3.

Chapter III

RESTITUTIO IN THE DECRETAL LAW

Article I. REQUISIVIT—the first Decretal on Restitutio in Integrum

It was by means of the decretals that *restitutio in integrum* became a recognized legal remedy in canonical procedure. It was in a decretal of uncertain date sent by Alexander III (1159-1181) to the Bishop of Alife, in the province of Benevento, Italy, that the first legislation of consequence regarding this remedy appeared.[1] This decretal had a twofold importance: a) it extended the remedy to include the Church under the subject of *restitutio in integrum,* and b) it first introduced it into ecclesiastical law in an authentic source.

Though the text nowhere employs the phrase *restitutio in integrum* or even any form of the verb *restituere,* the intention of Pope Alexander to rescind the contract by *restitutio* and not on any other ground is clear from his statement *ecclesia iure minoris debeat semper illaesa servari.* The church had made no provision to protect minors from being damaged; but in Roman law they were protected by this remedy; the Pope in stating that the church had the rights of minors meant that in this case it had the right to *restitutio in integrum.* He rescinded the contract, placing both parties in their previous state as if they had not entered into the contract; he insisted that the church

[1] "Requisivit a nobis tua fraternitas, quid agendum sit de possessionibus sub modico censu concessis? Noveris itaque, quod, si ecclesia laesa est, et manifeste apparet detrimentum ipsius, quum episcopo eiusdem ecclesiae conditionem facere deteriorem non liceat, et ecclesia iure minoris debeat semper illaesa servari, quae in damnum eius data constiterit ad ipsius convenit ius proprietatem redire. Providendum est, tamen, ne, si forte coloni possessiones illas expensis ac labore suo reddiderent meliores, sumptibus, quos bona fide fecerunt, debeant defraudari."—c. 1, X, *de in integrum restitutione,* I, 41. Jaffé assigns no date—*Regesta Pontificum Romanorum ab condita ecclesia ad annum post Christum natum MCXCVIII* (2. ed., 2 vols., Lipsiae, 1881-1888), n. 13737.

should not emerge in a better condition by enjoining that the other party to the contract be repaid for any improvements made on the property. He spoke of the *detrimentum* which the church had manifestly suffered to show that the damage required for *restitutio* in Roman law was present.

Minors had been perhaps the first and certainly the most frequent beneficiaries of this remedy in Roman law. The Roman republic itself could invoke the remedy because it enjoyed the rights of minors.[2] Following the Gloss, Hostiensis (+ 1271) in his commentary says that the Church enjoys the rights of minors because it is a republic; he finds this equation of church and state in St. Augustine by greatly straining a text [3] and in an enactment of the Emperor Justinian which required a period of one hundred years for the prescription of church property.[4] Though there were, through the centuries, repeated enactments on the alienation of church property to provide that the church be kept *semper illaesa,* this is apparently the first statement of the fact that it is to be protected *iure minoris.* In the beginning almost any alienation of church property had been forbidden except as the needs of the poor demanded it.[5] Alienation in opposition to the canonical prohibitions was either declared null [6] or to be revoked, the transaction being rescinded.[7] No council,

[2] C. (1, 50) 1; (11, 30) 3.

[3] *Super Ioannem,* tract. L, ad c. 12, n. 10—*MPL,* XXV, 1762; c. 3, C. XXIII, q. 4.

[4] C. (1, 2) 23. Cf. Hostiensis (Henricus de Segusio), *In Quinque Libros Decretalium Commentaria* (5 vols., Venetiis, 1581), I, *h. t.,* "Ecclesia," n. 2; Durantis cites the same texts—*Speculum Iuris,* lib. II, partic. III, *h. t.,* § 4, n. 3.

[5] Cf. can. 15, Council of Ancyra (314)—Harduin, I, 278; *Constitutiones Apostolorum,* VIII, 47; 38—Funk, *op. cit.,* I, 575; in Roman law, N. (7, pr.-1). Cf. Cleary, *Canonical Limitations on the Alienation of Church Property,* Catholic University of America Canon Law Studies, n. 100 (Washington: Catholic University of America, 1936), pp. 16, 23-25.

[6] Council of Epaon (517), can. 7—Bruns, *Canones Apostolorum et Conciliorum saeculorum IV—V—VI—VII* (2 vols., Berolini, 1939), II, 168; III Synod of Rome (502), can. 8—Harduin, II, 980.

[7] Council of Ancyra (314), can. 14—Harduin, I, 278; III Council of Orleans (538), can. 12—Bruns, II, 195.

however, stated that this rescinding was to be accomplished by a *restitutio in integrum.* The early discipline was gradually mitigated so that alienation was possible as long as a just cause was present and certain formalities were observed.[8] In the case contemplated in the *Requisivit* it was assumed that the solemnities had been observed so that the transaction was valid. For *restitutio* under Roman law was needed only against a valid act.

This first decretal on the extraordinary remedy came from the pen of a Pope who knew well the Roman law as well as the preceding canon law. For Rolandus Bandinelli, before he went to Rome and attained the positions that led him to the papacy as Alexander III, had taught the law at Bologna; before that he had been a pupil of Gratian. But credit for the recognition of *restitutio in integrum* is also greatly due to Bernard of Pavia (+ 1216). While he was provost of the cathedral at Pavia (1187-1191), Bernard made a collection of decretals, intending to fill any gaps left by Gratian and to include the decretals of the half century since the *Decretum.* Among these last was the *Requisivit,* a single chapter under the title *De in integrum restitutione ecclesiae vel minoris.*[9] This decretal had also been included in a collection made perhaps a year or two earlier, called the *Appendix Concilii Lateranensis III* because it was usually added to the canons of that council.[10] But there it appeared under the title "Concerning the Alienation of Church Property." [11] It remained for Bernard of Pavia, who followed the arrangement of the great collections of Roman law,[12] to rescue this decretal and stress the fact that it was not merely another prohibition of alienation but a case of *restitutio in integrum.* Preceding it he placed the title on acts vitiated by force and fear, much after the manner of Justinian's Digest.

[8] Cf. Cleary, *op. cit.,* p. 39 ff.

[9] I Compilatio, I, 31—*Antiquae Collectiones Decretalium cum Antonii Augustini Episcopi Ilerdensis notis* (Ilerdae, 1576)

[10] Cf. Van Hove, *Prolegomena,* n. 195.

[11] Pars XVI, c. 7—Mansi, XXII, 381.

[12] Tardif, *Histoire des Sources du Droit Canonique* (Paris, 1887), p. 187.

Because of the recognition received by this private collection of Bernard's—it became known as the First Compilation in spite of the fact that others had preceded it—the *Requisivit* did not need to wait until its inclusion in the authentic collection of Gregory IX to be used as an authority. Many Glosses and *Summae* served to spread the fame and use of this first compilation.[13] Of the *Ordines Iudiciarii,* however, which appeared about this time only that one which for a considerable time was ascribed to Roffredus Beneventanus cites this decretal.[14] Richardus Anglicus (+ 1237), though he used the first compilation elsewhere in his *Ordo* (c. 1196), in his treatment of *restitutio* cites only Roman law sources.[15] Likewise Damasus of Bologna, in speaking of this remedy in his *Summa de ordine iudiciario* (1210-1216), cited only the third compilation and did not speak of the use of the remedy as applied to the Church.[16]

Article II. The Law of the Decretals

Once *restitutio in integrum* had been established by Alexander III as a definite means of attacking a valid contract or sentence in the ecclesiastical court, it came into frequent use. The glossarists on the compilation of Bernard of Pavia immediately recurred to Roman law for its definition and the conditions, reasons,

[13] Kuttner lists those of Bernard himself, Petrus Hispanus, Richardus Anglicus, Alanus, Laurentius, Vincentius Hispanus, and Tancredus before the appearance of Gregory's decretals—*Repertorium der Kanonistik (1140-1234), Prodromus Corporis Glossarum,* I, Studi e Testi, n. 71 (Citta del Vaticano: Biblioteca Apostolica Vaticana, 1937), pp. 323-328.

[14] *Tractatus in quo ordines iudiciarii positiones libellique pertractantur* (Lugduni, 1561), p. 353, G. Though this work was completed in 1237, therefore after the Decretals of Gregory IX, this title is cited as it appeared in the first compilation.

[15] C. XLI, "De Officio Iudicis"—Wahrmund, *Quellen zur Geschichte des Römisch-Kanonischen Processes im Mittelalter* (Innsbruck: Verlag der Wagner'schen Universitäts-Buchhandlung., 1905 ——), Band II, Heft III, 112-113.

[16] Wunderlich, *Anecdota quae Processum Civilem Spectant (Bulgarus—Damasus—Bonaguida)* (Gottingae, 1841), tit 85.

and the time limit for its being granted.[17] But doubts and difficulties arose so that the Popes were asked to solve problems concerning the remedy; they were also asked to grant it in particular cases. As a result, a number of decretal letters were written on this subject by the Popes of the twelfth and thirteenth centuries, notably by Innocent III (1198-1216). Some of these decretals were included in the last three compilation.[18] By the time of the promulgation of the authentic collection of Decretals of Gregory IX (Sept. 5, 1234), there was a complete body of canonical legislation which included the essential features of the Roman institution as well as some which were distinctly canonical.[19]

Since no Pope defined *restitutio in integrum* in using the term, the Gloss devised a working definition: *In integrum restitutio est prioris status vel iuris redintegratio,* which has been commonly used ever since. Only later canonists gave more exhaustive definitions by piecing together the complete legislation of the decretals. This "restoration of the previous status or right" could be claimed either in judicial or extra-judicial matters; that is, either against business transactions, such as contracts,[20] or in court proceedings, especially against the judicial sentence.[21]

Restitutio was not considered in the strict sense an *actio,* a right of seeking by a judicial process that which is one's due.[22] It is referred to in the decretals as a *beneficium* or an *auxilium;* it becomes a right to judicial aid only in certain cases and through

[17] Cf. Bernardus Papiensis, *Summa Decretalium,* ed. Laspeyres (Ratisbonae, 1860), I, tit. 31, where he cites Justinian's Digest and Code.

[18] *III Compilatio,* I, 24; *IV Compilatio,* I, 17; *V Compilatio,* I, 23.

[19] Cc. 1-10, X, *de in integrum restitutione,* I, 41.

[20] Cc. 1, 8, X, *de in integrum restitutione,* I, 41.

[21] Cc. 3, 6, X, *de in integrum restitutione,* I, 41.

[22] Inst. (4, 6) pr. For this reason the Gloss at the beginning of the title on *restitutio* is inexact when it states that the preceding title, *De his, quae vi metusve causa fiunt,* contains specific uses of the generic remedy, *restitutio in integrum.* The Gloss on the Decretals of Boniface VIII (at the beginning of I, 21, in VI°) more correctly distinguishes the two titles; the one on force and fear refers to actions, while the one on *restitutio* refers to this extraordinary remedy which is not an action.

the concession of the legislator. It is, then, an extraordinary remedy to be used only when there is no ordinary remedy available to the plaintiff. For this reason writers quote the adage: *Habenti ordinarium remedium, non est tribuendum extraordinarium.*[23] Therefore, if an appeal from a sentence or an action for declaring the nullity of a contract or for its rescission were possible, *restitutio in integrum* was not to be sought. There was an exception made, however, for the sake of minors and the adage cited was modified *nisi sit pinguius ordinario.* Since this remedy was intended chiefly for privileged parties, minors and the Church, it was in a loose sense a privilege; it would have lost its privileged character if it had to be denied every time it concurred with an ordinary remedy which would not meet the situation so adequately.[24] For example, if a man who did not know the value of his farm sold it for less than half its just price, the choice was given to the buyer of making up the just price or of returning the property.[25] This was an ordinary remedy at the option of the buyer; and the man who sold his farm could not demand *restitutio in integrum.* Yet, if a church or a minor were the seller, he could seek the extraordinary remedy if it were more advantageous.[26]

A. *Conditions for Obtaining*

Restitutio in integrum was granted only in cases of a valid and rescissible transaction or sentence from which serious detriment occured.

From the fact that this remedy was given only when no ordinary one was available, it followed that it could not be employed against an invalid act. For a null act could be attacked by an action for the declaration of its nullity. If the validity of the act was doubtful, an alternative petition was allowed. For

[23] Cf. D. (4, 4) 16, pr.; Reiffenstuel, *op. cit.,* I, tit. 41, n. 6.

[24] Cf. Reiffenstuel, *op. cit.,* I, tit. 41, nn. 6-8; Schmalzgrueber, *Ius Ecclesiasticum Universum* (5 vols. in 12, Romae, 1843-1845), lib. I, par. II, tit 41, n. 3.

[25] C. 3, X, *de emptione et venditione,* III, 17.

[26] Cf. c. 11, X, *de rebus ecclesiae alienandis vel non,* III, 13, and the Gloss on this text.

example: If the sentence is null, I ask that it be declared null; if it be valid, I ask for *restitutio in integrum*. The same applied to contracts.[27] Besides being valid the act had to be rescissible. This remedy was never granted against marriage or religious profession, which, once validly existing, cannot be rescinded. It was used, however, in trials concerning the separation of married couples.[28]

Moreover *restitutio* could be sought only against an act which occasioned damage for the party asking the remedy. This damage had to be grave. To this effect commentators recited the adage, *de minimis non curat praetor,* which, though based on Roman law, is not found in legal sources.[29] Panormitanus (+ 1453) required a *laesio enormis*[30] and Covarruvias (+ 1577) said that his opinion became common.[31] The Gloss, however, merely modified the word *detrimentum* of the *Requisivit* with the adjective *grave* and added *nam de minimis non curat praetor*. So too Hostiensis.[32] Panormitanus is hardly to be understood, then, as using the term "enormous damage" in the strict sense of the civil law, namely, a damage exceeding half the value of the object.[33] Doubtless a later writer, Prosper Fagnanus (+ 1678), interpreted him rightly when he made the adjectives "great" and "enormous" synonyms.[34]

The general rule was that the degree of damage required for the use of the remedy was left to the prudence of the judge.

[27] Pope Gregory IX instructed his delegated judges "vel venditionem praedictam . . . nullam nunciare, si in ea debita iuris solemnitas est omissa, vel si forsitan intervenerit . . . in integrum restituere studeatis"—c. 8, X, *de in integrum restitutione,* I, 41.

[28] C. 4, X, *de in integrum restitutione,* I, 41.

[29] It is based on D. (4, 1) 4.

[30] Nicolaus de Tudeschis (Abbas Panormitanus), *Commentaria in quinque Libros Decretalium* (8 vols., Venetiis, 1588), I, *h. t.,* c. 1, n. 2, and c. 5, n. 1.

[31] *Variorum Resolutionum Libri IV,* II, c. III, n. 11—*Opera Omnia* (2 vols., Antverpiae, 1628), II, 22.

[32] *Commentaria,* I, h. t., c. 1.

[33] C. (4, 44) 2.

[34] *Commentaria in Quinque Libros Decretalium* (6 vols., Romae, 1661), I, *h. t.,* c. *Requisivit,* n. 8.

In many cases of *restitutio,* indeed, the damage could not be measured in terms of money. And in any case the gravity of the injury sustained was relative, depending on the comparative affluence or poverty of the parties involved.[35]

B. *The Subject of the Remedy*

The more frequent subjects of this remedy were minors and the church; adults could receive it only under certain circumstances.

1) Minors, as in Roman law, were those under twenty-five years of age.[36] A youth attained his majority at the beginning of the first day of his twenty-sixth year. Eventually the civil statutes of various states changed the age of majority. In Naples in the seventeenth century it was 18 years;[37] and with a brief of May 29, 1638, Urban VIII allowed the city of Perugia to consider those over twenty as having the same legal capacity as those over 25 years of age.[38] Beyond the fact that this remedy was granted to minors in the ecclesiastical court, the decretal law is silent.[39] From earliest times the commentators turned to Roman law as supplementary in regard to the restrictions and conditions concerning minors.

2) Since the church enjoyed the rights of minors, it was a subject of *restitutio in integrum.*[40] From the cases in which

[35] Cf. Veranus, *Iuris Canonici Universi Commentarius Paratitlaris* (5 vols., Monachii, 1703-1708), 1, tit. 41, No. I, n. 2.

[36] Prior to the present law of canon 88, § 1, there was no set age of majority. Like Roman law, the canon law referred to *minores XXV annis* and *maiores XXV annis,* retaining the comparative sense of the term. Different acts required different ages. A donation made by a person over 14 was binding and such a person could also be plaintiff in court without representation—c. 3, X, *de iudiciis,* II, 1, in VI°; c. 8, X, *de probationibus,* II, 19. Other ages were set for sacred orders, but 25 was recognized as the age of majority with regard to this remedy.

[37] Cala, *Tractatus Absolutissimus de Feriis* (Neapoli, 1675), q. IV, n. 1221.

[38] Jovius, *De Solemnitatibus in Contractibus Minorum* (Parmae, 1715), p. 349; text of the brief, pp. 182-183.

[39] C. 8, X, *de in integrum restitutione,* I, 41.

[40] Cc. 1, 3, X, *de in integrum restitutione,* I, 41.

it was granted it is obvious that *ecclesia* in the texts means an individual church. And one church could make use of this remedy against another, just as one minor could against another.[41] Monasteries, convents, hospitals, and other pious houses also enjoyed this remedy, for the law considered them as equivalent to churches for other privileges.[42] But in spite of the fact that the property of clerics was considered as ecclesiastical property in some cases,[43] clerics did not personally enjoy the privilege of the church for this remedy. If a cleric were a minor, he could of course seek it as any other minor.

3) In order that those over twenty-five years of age could use this remedy, besides damage and the lack of other remedy a just cause was needed. As in Roman law, absence was considered the chief cause.[44] It was within the judge's discretion to decide whether there was a just cause for using the remedy.

C. *The Object of the Remedy*

This remedy could be invoked, as previously pointed out, in either judicial or extra-judicial matters. Regarding the latter the decretalists appealed to Roman law to demonstrate that *restitutio in integrum* was possible against any valid and rescissible transaction. The decretals themselves mention contracts without any limitation as to kind.[45] Minors did not need the remedy against prescription, since it did not run against them,[46]

[41] C. 3, X, *de in integrum restitutione,* I, 41.

[42] Cf. c. 2, X, *de in integrum restitutione,* I, 41; *V Compilatio,* I, 23, c. 2 —*Quinta Compilatio Epistolarum Decretalium Honorii III Pont. Max.*, ed. Cironius (Tolosae, 1645), pp. 63-64; c. 2, X, *de consuetudine,* I, 4.

[43] C. 58, C. XVI, q. 1; c. 4, X, *de immunitate ecclesiarum, coemeterii, et rerum ad eas pertinentium,* III, 49.

[44] C. 18, X, *de sententia et re iudicata,* II, 27; c. 4, X, *de in integrum restitutione,* I, 41. According to the latter text, however, when the petionerer had been absent from the trial through the fraud of the other party, one of the motives Pope Innocent III advanced in giving this remedy was "in favorem tamen matrimonii."

[45] C. 1, *de restitutione in integrum* I, 21, in VI°.

[46] C. (2, 40) 5, 1.

but it did run against the church,[47] which could, if damaged, invoke *restitutio.*[48]

The use of this remedy in judicial matters was likewise varied. It could be obtained to present proof after the lapse of time allowed peremptorily and in spite of the fact that a prorogation had already been denied;[49] or even to present proofs after the discussion of the case had been concluded and the sentence was awaited.[50]

The highly privileged character of *restitutio in integrum* as an extraordinary remedy appears, however, especially in its use after a judicial sentence had been pronounced. The sentence should ordinarily end litigation; but since judgments may be erroneous, remedies are allowed to attack the sentence. Chief among these is the appeal, an application to a higher court for a rehearing of the case. But appeal had to be made within ten days after the notification that the sentence was rendered; otherwise the sentence was said to become a *res iudicata;* then the case was considered closed and the sentence was presumed to correspond to the truth so that it could no longer be attacked by appeal.[51] Yet, even after the ten day period the loser in the suit might obtain a *restitutio in integrum* to restore him to his former position so that he could appeal.[52] Again, in some circumstances an appeal was prohibited. If a case were committed to a judge with the clause *appellatione remota,* no appeal was possible from his sentence,[53] but *restitutio* was available to reopen the case.[54] Nor could a person who lost a case because of his

[47] C. 8, X, *de praescriptione,* II, 26.

[48] Cf. Hostiensis, *Commentaria,* I, *h. t.,* c. 1, n. 2.

[49] C. 7, X, *de in integrum restitutione,* I, 41.

[50] C. 3, X, *de in integrum restitutione,* I, 41.

[51] C. 15, X, *de appellationibus, recusationibus, et relationibus,* II, 28; c. 13, X, *de sententia et re iudicata,* II, 27.

[52] C. 10, X, *de in integrum restitutione,* I, 41.

[53] C. 41, X, *de appellationibus, recusationibus, et relationibus,* II, 28.

[54] C. 4, X, *de in integrum restitutione,* I, 41. In this text the words *sublato cuiusvis appellationis obstaculo* were omitted from the authentic publication of the Decretals; but such *partes decisae* can be used as an aid to interpret the text unless they were omitted to deny legal force to them;

contumacy make an appeal;[55] but another hearing might be granted through the extraordinary remedy.[56]

The status of a *res iudicata* arose when three conforming sentences were pronounced by different courts.[57] There is no certain case in the decretals wherein a *restitutio* was granted against the *res iudicata* rising out of three conforming sentences. Those cases in which the Popes granted new hearings through this remedy are not always completely enough reported to show why this remedy was needed. In some cases no reason is apparent why an appeal was not in order; yet the Pope granted *restitutio in integrum*.[58] Later writers take it for granted that *restitutio* was possible against three conforming sentences.[59] And Innocent III did grant the remedy after two conforming sentences. In one case he notes among his motives for conceding it that the civil courts allowed by means of a *restitutio* another examination of a case after a twofold sentence.[60] It is also clear from the same case that the Pope would grant a restoration against his own sentence. Such a remedy was particularly needed against a papal sentence as there was no superior to receive an appeal; a new hearing by him was the only resort.

The appeal was employed against a sentence which was valid but considered unjust. In case the sentence was for some reason or other null, even though no appeal had been made, the decision had no force.[61] In the decretal law a sentence could be null for many reasons. Durantis (+ 1296), writing within the century

it is very likely that these were omitted with other words of this part of the text for the sake of brevity. Cf. Van Hove, *Prolegomena*, n. 206.

[55] C. 8, X, *de officio iudicis ordinarii*, I, 31.

[56] C. 18, X, *de sententia et re iudicata*, II, 27.

[57] Cc. 3, 9, X, *de appellationibus, recusationibus, et relationibus*, II, 28.

[58] Cf. c. 2, X, *de in integrum restitutione*, I, 41; c. 14, X, *de privilegiis*, V, 33. On the latter case the Gloss remarks that the sentence must not have been appealed in time, as otherwise the extraordinary remedy would not have been possible.

[59] Covarruvias, *Practicae Quaestiones*, n. 7—*Opera Omnia*, I, 476; Veranus, *Commentarius Paratitlaris*, I, tit. 41, n. 10.

[60] C. 5, X, *de in integrum restitutione*, I, 41; cf. also c. 4, *ibid.*

[61] C. 1, X, *de sententia et re iudicata*, II, 27.

of the Decretals of Gregory IX, gives a long list of defects which rendered a sentence invalid. He catalogued the causes of nullity under headings: defects in the judge, in his jurisdiction, in the litigants, in the time or place, in the cause, quality, mode, or injustice of the sentence. Under each generic cause he gave explicit examples from the Decretals, the Decretum, or Roman law.[62] If the sentence were null, it was to be attacked by an action for the declaration of its invalidity.[63]

Nevertheless, it was frequently doubtful whether the sentence was actually null. The sources of nullity were so numerous and some of them so subtle and others so disputed (as can be seen in the text of Durantis) that one was not certain if a sentence could be declared null. Then a cumulative petition was permitted. The libellus would ask for all remedies—plaint of nullity, appeal, and *restitutio in integrum.* Such cumulative petitions are found in the decretals themselves,[64] and Durantis, after noting arguments to the contrary, says that the Curia observed the practice of admitting them and that he himself, at the mandate of Clement IV (+ 1265), had frequently received them and passed upon them.[65]

If a petition for *restitutio* had been once refused, a second request would not be received unless new proofs had been found to show a pressing reason for its being granted.[66] But if the petitioner had not appealed from the sentence against which *restitutio in integrum* had been denied, he might yet seek the remedy to regain the right of making an appeal.[67] There is a great

[62] *Speculum Iuris,* II, partic. III, *de sententia,* § 8, nn. 1 ff.

[63] C. 1, *de sententia et re iudicata,* II, 11, in Clem.; cf. Durantis, *ibid.,* n. 27.

[64] C. 8, X, *de in integrum restitutione,* I, 41; c. 14, X, *de privilegiis,* V, 33.

[65] *Speculum Iuris,* II, partic. III, *de sententia,* § 8, *Juxta,* n. 27.

[66] C. 10, X, *de in integrum restitutione,* I, 41. Gregory IX said that such a request "could" be denied; the Gloss, followed by the commentators, interpreted this as meaning could and "should" be denied.

[67] This is the better interpretation of the text: "Beneficio restitutionis in integrum ecclesiae tunc in alio iudicio denegata, restitutionem, praeterquam

difference between obtaining this remedy against the sentence and obtaining it merely for an appeal. *Restitutio* against the sentence treated it as non-existing; *restitutio* to appeal allowed the sentence to stand while an appeal was made from it in ten days and prosecuted in the usual time and manner.

D. *Time Limit*

The availability of *restitutio in integrum* was limited to a period of four years. For minors this period began on the day they entered their twenty-sixth year; for the church and for adults it began with the cause of damage—the transaction or sentence.[68] Clement V (1305-1314) characterized this four year period as *tempus continuum.*[69] The Gloss on his text and also the subsequent writers explain that *continuum* is here used to include ferial days when judicial acts were forbidden, so that the time would run during 365 days a year; yet it is *tempus initio utile;* therefore the time would not begin to run immediately after the young man's twenty-fifth birthday or immediately after the damage if some other just impediment prevented the making of the request.[70] At first it was necessary not only that the petition for *restitutio in integrum* be made within the four years of grace, but also that the discussion of the case to grant

ad appellationem omissam, videtur posse negari"—c. 10, X, *de in integrum restitutione,* I, 41. It is, however, contrary to the summary of the chapter which reads: "restituitur tamen ad appellandum a sententia denegationis." Such a provision would be unnecessary; the refusal, since it was a new sentence in itself could be attacked by all possible remedies. The summaries of the chapters do not have the force of law and are not to be used for an interpretation contrary to the text (cf. Van Hove, *Prolegomena,* n. 206). Hostiensis interprets the text to mean that a *restitutio* could be obtained to appeal from the original sentence—*Commentaria,* I, *h. t.,* c. 10, n. 2; Reiffenstuel seems to hold both views at once—*op. cit.,* I, tit. 41, n. 41; Pirhing likewise appears contradictory—*Ius Canonicum in V Libros Decretalium* (5 vols., Dilingae, 1874-1877), I, tit. 41, nn. 33-35.

[68] C. 1, *de restitutione in integrum,* I, 21, in VI°. Cf. Hostiensis, *Summa Aurea, h. t.,* n. 4.

[69] C. un., *de restitutione in integrum,* I, 11, in Clem.

[70] Cf. Reiffenstuel, *op. cit.,* I, tit. 41, nn. 59-61.

it be finished in that time.[71] If the decision were delayed through the fault of the judge or someone other than the petitioner, the case could be carried beyond the four year limit. But a custom arose against this requirement so that the hearing on a petition might run beyond the *quadriennium.*[72]

E. *Procedure*

Restitutio in integrum was to be sought from a competent judge. The general rule, "actor sequitur forum rei," [73] held true for it. Thus a person wishing to have a contract rescinded would present his plea to the judge having jurisdiction over the other party. It has been the almost constant doctrine that the church could seek this remedy in the ecclesiastical court.[74] Gonzalez-Tellez (+ 1649) raised some doubt, asserting that the secular court was the only competent one when a layman was convened in civil matters; his opinion did not prevail.[75] *Restitutio* could be given by judges having ordinary jurisdiction together with administration, e. g., by bishops. Rectors of seminaries and many others had jurisdiction over persons but no territorial administration; therefore they could not grant this extraordinary remedy. Those who could themselves grant it could also delegate another judge to consider the petition for it as a principal case. Like those judges who had jurisdiction without administration and their delegated judges, arbiters could give a *restitutio in*

[71] C. un., *de restitutione in integrum*, I, 11, in Clem.; cf. the Gloss on this text and Panormitanus, *Commentaria,* h. t. (I, 11), in Clem, c. un., n.6.

[72] Barbosa (+ 1649) states that this custom was established by the time of Rebuff (+ 1557)—*Collectanea Doctorum tam Veterum quam Recentiorum in Ius Pontificium Universum* (5 vols., Lugduni, 1656), I, 11, c. un., in Clem, n. 4—IV, 405.

[73] C. 8, X, *de foro competenti,* II, 2.

[74] Cf. Panormitanus, *Commentaria,* III, *de rebus ecclesiae,* c. 11; *ibid.,* I, h. t., c. 1, n. 8, where he cites Innocent IV (1243-1254) as holding the same opinion; Reiffenstuel, *op. cit.,* II, tit. 2, n. 153; Wernz, *Ius Decretalium,* V, n. 732.

[75] *Commentaria Perpetua in Singulos Textus Quinque Librorum Decretalium Gregorii IX* (5 vols., Venetiis, 1699), I, tit. 41, c. 1, n. 2.

integrum only if it came up as an incidental question in a case over which they were competent.[76] The Roman law principle that a minor judge could not grant this remedy against the sentence of a superior judge was adopted by the commentators. In the decretals there was no law restricting a judge who had just rendered a sentence from considering a petition for this remedy against it. If he decided to allow the *restitutio,* he would then proceed to retry the case. Later a custom having the force of law grew up prohibiting a judge from rescinding his own sentence by *restitutio;* the petition had to go to the court of appeal or to the Holy See.[77]

The bare essentials of procedure were required for the discussion of a petition for *restitutio in integrum;* these were the presence of the parties and some examination of the case.[78] A *contestatio litis* was necessary for the validity of the proceedings if this remedy were the principal issue at stake.[79] It might also be required in other cases. Panormitanus gave the rule that a libellus should be presented and a joinder of issue made a) when the *restitutio* was the principal issue; b) when it was sought against a certain person; and c) when a fuller examination of the case was needed.[80] A petition to rescind a contract, then, always required a *contestatio litis;* but for a petition to present new proofs after the conclusion of the case none was needed.

In the examination of the case before the judge the damage suffered had to be proved if it were not manifest; likewise proof of minority might be required if that were the ground for seeking the remedy. And in the case of adults the presence of a

[76] C. 9, X, *de in integrum restitutione,* I, 41. Panormitanus gives the clearest explanation of the difficult terms of this decretal in his commentary on the text; cf. also Wernz, *Ius Decretalium,* V, n. 732, note 16.

[77] Cf. Bouix, *Tractatus de Iudiciis Ecclesiasticis* (2. ed., 2 vols., Parisiis, 1855), II, 419.

[78] ". . . partibus praesentibus decernatur, quorum assertione merita causarum panduntur"—c. 5, X, *de in integrum restitutione,* I, 41.

[79] C. 2, X, *de officio iudicis,* I, 32; c. 2, X, *ut lite non contestata non procedatur ad testium receptionem vel ad sententiam definitivam,* II, 6.

[80] *Commentaria,* I, *de officio iudicis,* c. 2, n. 7.

just cause needed to be established. For a procurator to request a *restitutio in integrum* a special mandate was needed unless he sought the remedy as incidental to the case of his client or unless he had a general mandate.[81]

When *restitutio* was sought against a judicial sentence, it was customary to consider the question of the remedy itself separately; then, if it were granted, to proceed to the retrial of the principal question.[82] If the petitioner sought to rescind a contract, the two discussions proceeded together, the proofs which were adduced to obtain the *restitutio in integrum* which rescinded the contract serving also to obtain the restoration of the object of the contract.[83]

F. *Effects*

Many of the particular effects of *restitutio* have necessarily been already noted in the treatment of its conditions, subject, object, and procedure. The general effect of it was that the act—either a transaction or a sentence—was rescinded and treated as if it had never existed. All parties concerned were restored to their previous conditions. If a church had traded a farm for ten horses and then received this remedy against the deal because of the detriment it suffered, the church would receive its farm again; and the other party would receive his horses. Both had to be restored to their first condition, not to a better one. Such a restoration entailed the return of any fruits that had accrued to either side.[84] If the *restitutio in integrum* were granted against a sentence, the parties stood as they did at the beginning of the trial. The acts of the process were

[81] C. 7, X, *de in integrum restitutione,* I, 41; cf. Panormitanus, *Commentaria,* I, h. t., c. 6, n. 5.

[82] Cf. c. 5, X, *de in integrum restitutione,* I, 41.

[83] Hostiensis has much on the procedure of his time concerning this remedy—*Commentaria,* I, *h. t.,* c. 5, nn. 19-22.

[84] In granting one *restitutio,* Innocent III restored a villa to a monastery which had sold it too cheaply to pay off its debts; but he ordered the fruits to be retained by the buyer—c. 11, X, *de rebus ecclesiae alienandis vel non,* III, 13.

therefore discarded. If the remedy were granted merely to make possible the lodging of an appeal, the sentence and also the acts of the first trial still stood.

Ordinarily when *restitutio* was granted against a sentence, there would be no execution of the sentence while either the question of the remedy or the ensuing retrial pended. If there were a suspicion of malice on the part of the person seeking the new hearing, but yet there was sufficient cause for granting the remedy, the judge might order the sentence to be executed; in this case he would require the party in whose favor the sentence had been pronounced to put up a guaranty that he would carry out the provisions of the new sentence if the case went against him.

[85] Cf. c. 6, *de in integrum restitutione,* I, 41.

Chapter IV

FROM THE DECRETALS TO THE CODE OF CANON LAW

The law on *restitutio in integrum* became fixed in the decretals. Between the publication of the Decretals of Clement V (1317) and the appearance of the Code of Canon Law no legislation of a fundamental nature regarding this remedy was enacted. The Council of Trent (1545-1563) indeed regulated court procedure in some respects, particularly the related matter of appeals, but not in so detailed a manner as to consider the extraordinary remedies to be used in their stead.[1] Changes that were wrought in this institution after the time of the decretals were brought about rather through practice than through legislation. Though all phases of this development might be considered together, for the sake of clarity it will be better to isolate two particular cases to which this remedy was adapted in the course of time—causes concerning religious profession and the bond of matrimony. *Restitutio in integrum* was of course useless against the religious profession or the marriage itself; these two acts, once validly posited, are irrevocable. But under certain circumstances it became necessary to recur to *restitutio* to have their doubtful validity discussed in court. Upon an examination of this extraordinary remedy in these two types of cases there must follow some consideration of the general practice of the Roman Curia in regard to it.

Article I. Religious Profession

The Council of Trent determined that a religious who wished to assert the nullity of his profession because of force and fear or for lack of canonical age or in view of similar cause should be given a hearing only within five years of the date of his profession.[2] If the religious made no attempt to have his

[1] Cf. sess. XIII, *de ref.*, c. 7; sess. XXII, *de ref.*, cc. 1-3; sess. XXIV, *de ref.*, c. 20.

[2] "Quicumque regularis praetendat, se per vim et metum ingressum esse

profession declared invalid in five years, it was presumed that he had renewed his consent so that the profession became valid. No exception was made in the law for the case in which it was physically or morally impossible to call the validity of the profession into question during the five years. But apparently some bishops contined to try these cases if the religious had not been able to present his case in the time permitted. Gregory XIII, therefore, at the request of the Sacred Congregation of the Council, declared that no religious was to be heard concerning the nullity of his profession even if he alleged that the force and fear had continued throughout the five year period.[3]

By 1650, however, the Sacred Congregation of the Council began to allow cases on religious profession to be introduced after five years from the day of profession by means of a *restitutio in integrum,* reserving to the Holy See the right to grant such a restoration against the lapse of time.[4] This custom which had grown up in the Sacred Congregation of the Council was sanctioned by Benedict XIV (1740-1758) in his Constitution *Si datam* on March 4, 1748. He reasserted the fact that the remedy could be obtained only from the Holy See, declared the Sacred Congregations of the Council and of Bishops and Regulars and also the Rota to be competent in the matter.[5]

religionem; aut etiam dicat, ante aetatem debitam professum fuisse, aut quid simile; velitque habitum dimittere quacumque de causa; aut etiam cum habitu discedere sine licentia superioris, non audiantur, nisi intra quinquennium tantum a die professionis."—Sess. XXV, *de regularibus, c.* 19.

[3] The only record of this decree is apparently its citation by the S. Congregation of the Council in a decision of March 5, 1598, as reported in Pallottini, *Collectio omnium conclusionum et Resolutionum S. C. Concilii ab anno 1564 ad annum 1860* (17 vols., Romae, 1867-1893), *s. v.,* "Professio religiosa," § VII, n. 2

[4] Cf. Pallottini, *op. cit., s. v.* "Professio religiosa," § VII, nn. 4, 6, 47, *et passim.* It seems the remedy was not yet made available at the time of Sanchez (+ 1610); he argued for its possibility but did not mention the fact that it was granted by the Congregation—*De Sancto Matrimonii Sacramento* (3 vols., Lugduni, 1659), lib. VII, disp. 37, nn. 21-23.

[5] §§ 17-21—*Codicis Iuris Canonici Fontes,* cura Emi. Petri Card. Gasparri

In the beginning the Sacred Congregation of the Council had granted the *restitutio* as a matter of form without much pomp of procedure. It became the custom, however, to examine the principal issue of the nullity of the profession together with the question of granting the extraordinary remedy. If there were no solid ground for asserting the invalidity of the profession, the remedy would not be granted; if it were conceded, then the examination of the principal cause by the delegated judges was merely a ceremonial affair.[6] Benedict XIV commended the Congregation for its care in examining these cases and enjoined all courts considering the causes for a *restitutio in integrum* in the matter of religious profession to use the same care in the future.[7] By the nineteenth century the Sacred Congregation of Bishops and Regulars became the more usual agency for these cases.[8]

This use of *restitutio in integrum* was suppressed by the Code of Canon Law. Like other cases respecting the status of persons, a case concerning the validity of religious profession never becomes irrevocably adjudged and can be reopened whenever there is new evidence to prompt such action.[9] A profession that was null in the beginning because of an external impediment is not revalidated by a renewal of consent, no matter how much time elapses from the date of profession.[10]

Article II. Marriage Cases

The sentence in a matrimonial case enjoyed the privilege of never becoming irrevocably adjudged because the enforcing of

editi, vols. 1-6 (Romae, 1922-1932); cura Emi. Iustiniani Card. Serédi, vols. 7-9 (Romae, 1935-1939), n. 385. Hereafter cited as *Fontes*.

6 De Luca, *De Regularibus*, disc. 41, n. 13— *Theatrum Veritatis et Iustitiae* (16 vols., Coloniae Agrippinae, 1706).

7 Const. "*Si datam,*" § 20—*Fontes*, n. 385.

8 Pallottini (*op. cit., s. v.*, "Professio religiosa," § VII) lists over two hundred cases of the seventeenth and eighteenth century, none of the nineteenth; the *Collectanea Sacrae Congregationis Episcoporum et Regularium* (Romae, 1885) shows only nineteenth century cases; cf. e. g., pp. 146, 157.

9 Canon 1903.

10 Canon 586.

an erroneous sentence might entail the occasion of sin.[11] Yet it was recognized, at least from the time of Panormitanus (+ 1453)[12] that one should not be allowed to ask for rehearings of a case indefinitely; if the sentence were not appealed in ten days or if two or perhaps three sentences were pronounced in favor of the validity of the marriage, the way of appeal was closed. The sentence had at least this effect of the *res iudicata.* It would not be reconsidered unless new allegations were made to convince the judge that the sentence might be erroneous. This view was approved and given legal force by Benedict XIV in his Constitution *Dei Miseratione.*[13]

Since the way of appeal was closed, Hostiensis held that a matrimonial case could be reopened by either a *restitutio in integrum* or a *supplicatio.* This latter remedy was a petition made only to the Pope to ask that he gratuitously allow the case to be retried. This involved an entirely new process, while a *restitutio in integrum ad audientiam,* according to Hostiensis, allowed a new hearing in which the previous libellus, citations, and testimony could again be employed.[14] Panormitanus admitted the possibility of a *restitutio in integrum* with the same effect; but instead of a *supplicatio* he spoke of a *querela.*[15] Later writers do not speak of any request for a *restitutio* to obtain a rehearing, but only of the *querela.* This resembled supplication; it was directed not to the Pope nor to the appellate judge, but to the judge who had rendered the sentence; and while supplication was founded on an error committed by the judge, the *querela* was founded on the error of the party himself or on the fraud

[11] Cf. c. 7, X, *de sententia et re iudicata,* II, 27, and the Gloss on the text. For distinctions between sentences which thus did not become a *res iudicata* and those in some marriage cases which did, because they would not foster a sinful union, cf. Hostiensis, *Commentaria,* I, *h. t.,* c. 4, n. 13; *Summa Aurea,* I, *de testibus,* n. 11; Sanchez, *De Sancto Matrimonii Sacramento,* lib. VII, disp. 100, nn. 4, 13; lib. X, disp., 9, nn. 4, 7.

[12] *Commentaria,* II, *de sententia et re iudicata,* c. 7, n. 9.

[13] 3 nov. 1741, § 11—*Fontes,* n. 318.

[14] *Commentaria,* I, *h. t.,* c. 4, n. 13.

[15] *Commentaria,* I, *h. t.,* c. 4, n. 13.

of the other party.[16] Reiffenstuel held that the judge, upon receiving the *querela*, had to grant a *restitutio in integrum* if the hearing of the case was to be made possible; he remarked, however, that Panormitanus, in speaking of the *querela*, made no mention of the *restitutio* which followed it. Neither, however, did Reiffenstuel's contemporaries, who wrote as if the mere acceptance of the *querela* were enough to make possible a retrial of the case.[17]

All this is merely of a doctrinal nature. It is difficult to ascertain what the practice of the Sacred Congregation of the Council was during the centuries; it did not apparently mention *restitutio in integrum* in allowing new hearings of marriage cases until the last century. Whether a *restitutio* or merely a new hearing on the strength of the *querela* was granted is of slight import. Authors are unanimous in their teaching that to present a *querela* new and forceful documents or witnesses were necessary; but these were sufficient also for granting the extraordinary remedy; its use in such a case against a sentence which was not irrevocably adjudged was but a formality.

After the restoration of the Rota in 1908 the first reported case which bears on this point was one from Baltimore in 1911. The case had been twice decided in favor of the validity of the marriage. The Rota, quoting Reiffenstuel, said *solum possit retractari per viam querelae,* without any mention of *restitutio in integrum.*[18] That this extraordinary remedy became definitely useless to reintroduce a marriage case with the advent of the Code of Canon Law can best be seen from a case decided by the Supreme Tribunal of the Signatura soon after the publication

[16] Scaccia gives these two distinctions between the remedies, but he also notes that *supplicatio, querela, recursus, reclamatio,* and *revisio* were usually employed promiscuously—*Tractatus de Appellationibus* (3. ed., Coloniae, 1717), q. XVIII, n. 30.

[17] Reiffenstuel, *op. cit.,* II, tit. 27, n. 138; cf. Pirhing, *Ius Canonicum,* II, tit. 27, nn. 51-52; Leurenius, *Forum Ecclesiasticum* (5 vols, Venetiis, 1729), IV, q. 257, n. 3.

[18] *Baltimoren. nullitatis matrimonii,* 29 nov. 1911, dec. XLIII, n. 2—*Decisiones,* III (1911), 502.

of the Code. Remarking that matrimonial cases never become irrevocably adjudged, the Signatura decided that there was no place for a *restitutio in integrum* in such a case since it was, according to canon 1905, an extraordinary remedy to be used especially against a sentence which had become a *res iudicata.*[19]

Article III. The Practice of the Roman Curia

The practice or the mode of action of the Congregations and Tribunals of the Roman Curia has long been both a norm of action for other ecclesiastical tribunals and a source of general law. Of particular importance with reference to *restitutio in integrum* are the regulations set up at various times by the Popes for the Roman tribunals. No specific mention is made of *restitutio* in the many papal documents regarding the Sacred Roman Rota until Pius IV (1559-1565) reorganized that tribunal in 1561. He merely declared that an Auditor of a case might set a time for hearing a petition for this remedy without a new commission.[20] Later Paul V (1605-1621) allowed the rotal judges to grant the remedy even beyond the four year time limit if they saw fit.[21]

That *restitutio in integrum* was in frequent use with the Rota from the sixteenth through the eighteenth century can be seen by a glance at any of the numerous volumes of Rota decisions published during this period. The *dubium* often placed before the judges was worded: *"An constet de re iudicata seu potius de causis restitutionis in integrum in casu?"* It became the custom to attack a sentence which was believed to be invalid or unjust by means of a *restitutio.* The injustice or nullity of the sentence was considered the damage necessary for using this remedy.[22]

[19] *Paderbornen, nullitatis matrimonii,* 31 nov. 1919—*AAS,* XI (1919), 295-297.

[20] Const. *"In throno iustitiae,"* 27 dec. 1561, § 2—*Bull. Rom.,* VII, 155.

[21] Const. "Universi agri," 1 mart. 1612, § V, n. 4—*Bull. Rom.,* XII, 68.

[22] Cf., e. g., *Decisiones Recentiores*: I, dec. 492, n. 1 (May 24, 1613); XVIII, tom. 2, dec. 593, n. 5 (July 1, 1695); *ibid.,* dec. 740, n. 1 (June 19, 1676); also *Decisiones Coram Pianetti* (Viterbii, 1839-1840), dec. 9, n. 7 (June 8, 1821).

The result was that the plaint of nullity was practically forgotten as a remedy against an invalid sentence for the sake of this extraordinary one. Cardinal De Luca (+ 1638) testifiies: "Thus very often, and almost thousands of times I have disputed at the Rota on the accustomed question: *'an constet de re iudicata vel potius de causis restitutionis in integrum;'* never indeed have I disputed nor have I seen it disputed principally on the question: *'an constet de nullitatibus'*." [23]

Of the Signatura's use of *restitutio* before the nineteenth century little is known. When Pius VII (1800-1823) reformed the administrative and judicial system of the Papal States in 1816, he laid down specific grounds for which the Signatura could grant the remedy against an irrevocably adjudged sentence. Either new documents had to be discovered which decisively proved new facts, or the sentence had to be unjust because some law was neglected or violated in the trial.[24] This latter reason for impeaching a sentence of injustice was adopted from the French court of cassation which functioned during the French invasion of Italy.[25] In 1834 Gregory XVI (1831-1846) revised the rules for the courts of the papal territories with his *"Regolamento legislativo e giudiciario,"* in which he gave more attention to *restitutio in integrum.*[26]

According to Gregory's *Regolamento* there was granted the possibility of recourse for *restitutio in integrum* to the Signatura against a sentence of the Rota when the petitioner could establish the manifest injustice of the sentence. This manifest in-

[23] *De Iudiciis,* disc. 38, n. 5. De Luca condemned the ease with which the Rota granted *restitutio—Ibid.,* nn. 11-12.

[24] Motu proprio *"Reformatio publicae administrationis et tribunalium ditionis Ponticiae,"* 6 iulii 1816, art. 53—*Bull. Rom. Cont.,* XIV, 53. This was substantially repeated by Leo XII—Motu proprio, *"Reformatio tribunalium Status Ecclesiastici,"* 5 oct. 1824, art. 50—*Bull. Rom. Cont.,* XVI, 134.

[25] Cf. Hanssen, "De Sanctione nullitatis in processu canonico," *Apollinaris,* XII (1939), 242. He cites the *"Regolamento organico della Giustizia civile e punitivo,"* 13 giulio 1806, art. 86-88, without source.

[26] *Acta Gregorii Papae* (4 vols., Romae, 1904), IV, 300-410.

justice could only result from 1) the sentence being pronounced because of documents that were later recognized to be false; 2) the finding of public or private documents which proved new and decisive facts; 3) the neglect of some law in the sentence; 4) the express contravention of some law in force.[27] The failure to observe the forms prescribed by the laws of procedure could be considered as violations of the law so as to allow the remedy only 1) if the tribunals did not give in writing the reason for doubting and deciding; 2) if the sentences were not juridically motivated; 3) if the substantial time limits—*termini*—of the trial were not observed.[28]

With the fall of the Papal States in 1870 both the Rota and the Signatura ceased to function as courts. In 1908 they were restored by Pius X (1903-1914) and a *Lex Propria* was published establishing the competence of each tribunal.[29] The competence of the Rota included the power to grant *restitutio* against the sentences of all lower tribunals; [30] the Signatura could grant it against a sentence of the Rota which had become irrevocably adjudged.[31] The *Regulae Servandae* of the Rota which were published in 1910 added nothing of import regarding this remedy, but the regulations of the Signatura, whose publication followed in 1912, changed the law of Gregory XVI concerning *restitutio in integrum*. Whereas the *Regolamento* allowed it for the neglect of a law or for the express violation of some law in force, the rules of the Signatura suppressed these two grounds for this remedy by making them rather the motives for a *querela nullitatis*.[32]

The regulations of the Signatura, however, added to the

[27] §§ 1057-1058.

[28] § 1059.

[29] Const. "*Sapienti consilio,*" 29 iun. 1908— *AAS,* I (1909), 15 ff.; *Fontes,* n. 682; *Lex Propria S. Romanae Rotae et Signaturae Apostolicae,* 29 iun. 1908—*AAS,* I (1909), 20-35; *Fontes,* n. 6459.

[30] *Lex Propria,* can. 14, n. 4— *AAS,* I (1909), 23, *Fontes,* n. 6459.

[31] *Lex Propria,* can. 37, n. 4—*AAS,* I (1909), 30; *Fontes,* n. 6459.

[32] Cf. *Regolamento,* § 1058—*Acta Gregorii Papae XVI,* IV, 365; *Regulae servandae in iudiciis apud Suprem. Signaturae Ap. Tribunal,* 6 mart. 1912, art. 4—*AAS,* IV (1912), 189; *Fontes,* n. 6462.

two remaining grounds for *restitutio*—the fact that the sentence was based on false documents and the finding of new and decisive documents—a third general cause. It read: *"Aut generatim rationem aliquam intercessisse non prius deductam neque disputatam, ex qua detrimentum grave atque manifestum boni iuris demonstrari queat, ideoque sit locus actioni rescissoriae, ad normam iuris communis."* [33] The interpretation of this broad provision was not without difficulty. For this reason the Prefect of the Signatura, Cardinal Lega, petitioned Pope Benedict XV (1914-1922) for an interpretation of the Supreme Tribunal's competence in the matter of the *querela nullitatis* and the *restitutio in integrum*. He explained the interpretation of the tribunal's competence as he felt it should be and asked a decision of the Pope. With a chirograph of June 28, 1915, Benedict approved the Signatura's competence as explained by Lega.[34]

As Lega pointed out, the jurisprudence of the Curia and the enactments of several Popes had confirmed the rule that a sentence is never null unless it be for the defect of citation, of competence, or of mandate. When a sentence of the Rota was attacked because of nullity before the Signatura, the question asked was: *"Sitne nulla rotalis sententia, et sitne loous eius circumscriptioni?"* [35] This was to be understood as a disjunctive and not as a copulative petition, Lega asserted. The declaration of nullity and the *circumscriptio* were two different things. Nullity could result only from three violations of positive law, but the sentence could be rescinded by *circumscriptio* if it manifestly sinned against the law or perverted the status of facts in the case. *Restitutio in integrum*, as a result, was to be invoked only when the sentence could be neither convicted of nullity nor "circumscribed." [36]

[33] Art. 9, c—*AAS*, I (1912), 190; *Fontes*, n. 6462.

[34] Benedict XV, chirographum *"Attentis expositis,"* 28 iun. 1915 (*Appendix ad regulas servandas in iudiciis apud Suprem. Signaturae Ap. Tribunal*, art. 1)—*AAS*, VII (1915), 320-325; *Fontes*, after n. 6462.

[35] *Lex Propria*, can. 41, § 3—*AAS*, I (1909), 31; *Fontes*, n. 6459.

[36] For a contemporary commentary on this chirograph, cf. *Le Canoniste Contemporain*, XXXVIII (1915), 420-421. Roberti (*De Processibus*, II, 252, note 1) says that, by virtue of the chirograph, petitioning for *circum-*

Historical Summary

Though the fully-developed Roman institution of *restitutio in integrum* was spoken of by some early ecclesiastical writers, the references are too infrequent and too uncertain to conclude that it was in use in church courts prior to the ninth century. Even when expositions of the remedy began to appear in the collections of law in the ninth century, they were either in non-canonical collections like the *Lex Romana Canonice Compta* or in sections of canonical works which referred perhaps exclusively to the civil courts, as in the *Decretum* of Ives of Chartres (+ 1116). The Decree of Gratian had nothing on the praetorian remedy of *restitutio,* though the term *in integrum restituere* or its equivalent is used in a loose sense several times.

The first canonical legislation of importance on the remedy was the decretal *Requisivit* of Alexander III (1159-1181) to the Bishop of Alife. The recognition of this decretal received impetus from the fact of its inclusion in the First Compilation by Bernard of Pavia (+ 1191). The Decretals of Gregory IX and the early commentaries upon them gave a complete romano-canonical legislation on *restitutio in integrum.*

After the Council of Trent *restitutio* was used to restore to a religious the right to attack the validity of his profession after the lapse of the five years from his profession which the Council allowed. It was also used at times to attack the sentence in a matrimonial case in spite of the fact that such a sentence did not become irrevocably adjudged. Both of these uses of the remedy became unnecessary with the advent of the Code of Canon Law.

The use of *restitutio in integrum* against the judicial sentence was both elaborated and restricted in the Roman tribunals, chiefly through the *Regolamento* of Gregory XVI in 1834, the *Lex Propria* of Pius X in 1908, and the *Regulae* of the Signatura in 1912.

scriptio meant asking for *restitutio.* But the document says of this latter remedy: "*. . . ita tamen ut sit locus huic actioni extraordinariae restitutoriae seu revocatoriae, quoties invocari non potest querela nullitatis aut actio rescissoria, de qua supra.*" The *actio de qua supra* is *circumscriptio* which must be impossible before *restitutio* can be used.

PART TWO
Canonical Commentary
SECTION A. THE REMEDY IN GENERAL

Chapter V

DEFINITION

Restitutio in integrum was defined at the beginning of the consideration of its history. Now it is expedient to reexamine the definition given in the light of the Code of Canon Law.

Although no definition of the term *restitutio in integrum* is found in the Code, the classic definition, formulated long before the codification, can easily be seen in the fundamental canons on the remedy—canons 1687-1689. The definition was:

> *Restitutio in integrum* is an extraordinary remedy of the law by which a person who has been gravely damaged by a valid but rescissible act or transaction may, because of natural equity, be returned, through the ministry of a competent judge, to that status in which he was before being damaged.[1]

That *restitutio in integrum* is an extraordinary remedy for the benefit of those gravely damaged can be seen in canon 1687; the need of the ministry of a competent judge is stated in canon 1688; and the effects of the remedy as sketched in the definition are given in canon 1689. A complete explanation of the terms of this definition would therefore entail an exhaustive commentary on these three canons. Before one proceeds to a commentary on the canons, however, it will be helpful to explain the definition briefly in all its terms. *Restitutio in integrum* is:

1) "An extraordinary remedy of the law." It is a remedy, not a preventative, and comes into play only when damage al-

[1] Reiffenstuel, *op. cit.*, I, tit. 41, n. 3. The words "by a valid but rescissible act" have been added to Reiffenstuel's definition from canon 1687, § 1.

ready exists. It is in the strict sense neither a privilege nor an *actio*. It is not a privilege because it is not a favor outside of or contrary to the common law, but a benefit conceded by the law itself; it is only in the loose sense a privilege such as others granted in the Code.[2] Neither is it rightly an action, that is, a "right of seeking by judicial trial that which is one's due."[3] There is no strict right entitling one to be returned to one's previous condition; *restitutio* is a benefit of the law conceded through the "noble office" of the judge. Yet it is akin to the rescissory actions. It has the same effect and is thence treated in the Code together with them under Title V of the first part of Book IV, "Concerning actions and exceptions." But the heading to Chapter III of that title notes the distinction between *restitutio* and the actions when it reads "Concerning rescissory actions and *restitutio in integrum*," and canon 1687 calls *restitutio* not an action but a remedy.[4] Following the Roman law on rescissory actions, the law of the Code does not grant a rescissory action to protect a right; rather a right is conferred by the establishment of such an action.[5] Thus actions are set up to rescind acts which have been performed through force and fear, or fraud, or error.[6] No action is allowed to rescind an act merely because damage resulted from it. Yet, that equity may be better served, a remedy is provided in *restitutio in integrum*.

[2] Cf. Cicognani, *Canon Law,* authorized English version by J. O'Hara and F. Brennan (2. ed., Philadelphia: Dolphin Press, 1935), p. 781; Van Hove, "De notione privilegii per actum peculiarem concessi," *Jus Pontificium,* XVIII (1938), 268-269.

[3] "Ius persequendi iudicio quod sibi debetur"—Inst. (4, 6) pr.; cf. Roberti, *De Processibus,* I, 48-49.

[4] No provision for this remedy was made in the first two *Schemata* for the Code; some of those who criticized the *Schemata* added to the title *"De actionibus rescissoriis"* the words *"et restitutionis in integrum."* This reading, which would make the remedy an action, was changed to that of the Code. *Schema E* (can. 173) described the remedy as a *"quasi actio rescissioria extraordinaria"*—Roberti, *Codicis Iuris Canonici Schemata, Lib. IV De Processibus, I De Iudiciis in Genere* (Civitate Vaticana: Typis Polyglottis Vaticanis, Pont. Inst. Utriusque Iuris, 1940), p. 176, note 12; p. 178.

[5] Cf. Roberti, *De Processibus,* I, 381.

[6] Canons 1684-1686; cf. canons 103-104.

It is an "extraordinary" remedy, not that it is something remarkable, but a subsidiary or subordinate remedy over and above the ordinary ones.[7] It can be employed only when no other action or remedy of the law is possible.

It is an extraordinary remedy "of the law." Originally *restitutio* was a remedy of the magistrate, but even in Roman law it became rather a remedy granted by the law and it has always been such in canon law. It is not a personal concession of the judge; his office is but to apply the law to the particular case.

2) "By which a person." This remedy is the prerogative chiefly of minors and those who enjoy the same rights as minors, but it is available also to adults under certain conditions laid down in canon 1687, § 2. The "person" who can use *restitutio* will be more fully treated in the next chapter on "The Subject of the Remedy."

3) "Who has been gravely damaged." It has been noted that the foundation of this remedy is the damage suffered by a party.[8] It must be grave damage since canon 1687, § *1*, reads *graviter laesis.* Although in the old law disputes arose as to how great the damage had to be for this remedy—whether or not it must be *enorme,* that is, exceeding half the value of the object involved —the measure of grave damage is left to the discretion and prudence of the judge.[9] The gravity of damage is a relative matter. What would be grave damage for one would be slight for another. It must not be due to chance or ill fortune.[10] If a house which a minor purchased were struck by lightning and

[7] Cf. Pirhing, *Ius Canonicum,* I, tit. 41, n. 2; S. R. Rota, *De Manila, legatorum piorum,* 18 febr. 1919—*AAS,* XII (1920), 185.

[8] Cf. Pellegrini, *Praxis Vicariorum* (Venetiis, 1696), par. II, sect. II, subsect. 11, n. 9.

[9] Reiffenstuel, *op. cit.,* I, tit. 41, n. 8; Roberti, *De Processibus,* I, 388; Cocchi, *Commentarium in Codicem Iuris Canonici, Lib. IV De Processibus* (Taurinorum Augustae: Marietti, 1930), n. 96; S. R. Rota, *S. Iacobi de Chile, restitutionis in integrum et compromissi,* 5 iulii 1927, dec. XXXIV, n. 12—*Decisiones, XIX* (1927), 283.

[10] Coronata, *Institutiones,* III, n. 1216; Cocchi, *De Processibus,* n. 96.

burned down, he could not seek *restitutio* because of his loss. The damage must be due rather to the fraud of another person or to excusable ignorance or oversight or to an inability to defend one's rights because of absence or sickness.

4) "A valid but rescissible act." This remendy, like the rescissory actions, repairs damage caused by a valid but recissible act. Just what acts are to be included will be discussed in Chapter VI. The act must be valid, that is, recognized by the law as existing, for if it does not exist, it cannot be rescinded. Moreover, to be rescinded an act must be capable of rescission; a marriage contract, sacred ordination, or religious profession cannot be rescinded.

5) "Because of natural equity." This is the one term of the definition which nowhere appears explicitly in the canons on *restitutio in integrum*. Equity was the ground for this remedy in Roman [11] as well as in ecclesiastical law.[12] Now that the remedy is firmly established in the law, it is not necessary for the law itself to note that it is an institution based on equity. There is, however, still a trace of the fact that equity is the motive for *restitutio in integrum* even in the Code. Canon 1687, § 2, requires a righteous cause for the restoration of adults, and equity is operative only when such a righteous cause exists.[13] Equity, among the older writers, was defined as "justice tempered by the sweetness of mercy." [14] It was considered synonymous with *"equum et bonum."* [15]

6) "By which a person may be returned to that status in which he was before being damaged." The effects of the remedy will be considered more fully in Chapter VIII.

7) "Through the ministry of a competent judge." A person

[11] Cf. D. (4, 4) 1, pr.; 24, 1.

[12] C. 3, X, *de in integrum restitutione,* I, 41; cf. also commentators generally on the definition of the remedy.

[13] Reiffenstuel, *op. cit.,* I, tit. 41, n. 13.

[14] Panormitanus quotes this definition from Ioannes Andreae as that of St. Cyprian, noting that Durantis also used it—*Commentaria,* I, *De Transactionibus* (tit. 36), c. 11, n. 7; Reiffenstuel, *op. cit.,* I, tit. 2, n. 418. *"equum et bonum."* [15]

[15] Reiffenstuel, *ibid.,* n. 415; cf. D. (4, 4) 24, 1.

who has suffered damage cannot declare on his own authority the rescission of an act. Since the act is valid, it is binding unless rescinded by the proper authority. A party in presenting his petition to a judge can only ask for *restitutio,* retailing his grounds for seeking it. The competency of the judge as laid down in canon 1688, § 1, will be treated in Chapter VIII.

From these preliminary notions on the definition of *restitutio in integrum,* three essential conditions can be noted for its use: There must be 1) grave damage, 2) from a valid but rescissible act, and 3) a righteous cause for the remedy. These conditions are all required by canon 1687.

Although it will be necessary to speak frequently of the damage required in particular cases, no further treatment of this condition will be given *ex professo.* The next chapter will be devoted to "The Subject of the Remedy." In it the third condition, namely, the righteous cause, will be studied since the cause varies with the subject. In Chapter VII, on "The Object of the Remedy," the second condition, that the damage result from a valid but rescissible act, will be amplified. Finally, in Chapter VIII, on "The Remedy at Work," the time limit, the competent judge, and the manner of petitioning and conceding the remedy will be outlined in the discussion of canon 1688, together with the effects of the remedy as set forth in canon 1689.

Chapter VI

The Subject of the Remedy

Canon 1687.—§ 1. Minoribus vel minorum iure fruentibus graviter laesis eorumque heredibus et successoribus, ad laesionem reparandam ex negotio seu actu valido rescindibili praeter alia ordinaria remedia, suppetit remedium extraordinarium restitutionis in integrum.

§ 2. Hoc beneficium maioribus quoque conceditur quos deficit rescissoria actio aut aliud ordinarium remedium, dummodo iustam subesse causam et laesionem sibi imputandam non esse probaverint.

If *restitutio in integrum* is granted because of natural equity, it will be granted only when a righteous cause exists. At first sight canon 1687 requires such a cause only when an adult person wishes to use the remedy; the clause *dummodo iustam subesse causam probaverint* appears only in the second paragraph concerning adults; in the first paragraph of the canon, which deals with minors and those who enjoy their privileges, no mention is made of any cause. The reason for the difference is easily apparent. In the case of minors the existence of a righteous cause is taken for granted by the law; minority itself is sufficient cause. In the case of adults some other righteous cause is demanded. Minority may be said to be the ordinary cause for *restitutio,* while the causes which are of use to adults are extraordinary ones.[1] The cause required is an impediment of the moral or physical order which was responsible in some way for the damage and after its occurrence justifies the use of an extraordinary remedy.[2] It is a righteous cause specifically because it justifies the use of *restitutio in integrum.*

[1] Lega-Bartoccetti, *Commentarius in Iudiciis Ecclesiasticis iuxta Codicem Iuris Canonici* (2 vols., Romae: Anonima Libraria Cattolica Italiana, 1938-1939), I, 432.

[2] Roberti, *De Processibus,* I, 388.

Article I. Minors

A minor is a person who has not yet completed his twenty-first year.[3] Up to the Code the age of majority in canon law, following the Roman law computation, was set at twenty-five years for *restitutio* and other patrimonial affairs. Canon 88 of the Code defines the age of majority applicable throughout the law for the first time.[4] In reducing the age of majority to 21 years the Church followed the practice of many of the civil laws.[5] Majority is reached at the completion of the twenty-first year. Thus a person is considered a minor until the conclusion of the day which marks his twenty-first birthday; a child born on June 1, 1940, will attain his majority at midnight beginning June 2, 1961.[6]

At the age of 21 an individual is considered to have reached sufficient maturity to be able to exercise his rights fully and in his own name. Prior to that time he is subject to the power of his parents or tutors in the exercise of his rights, except in those cases in which the law exempts him from subjection to that power.[7] This subjection to parental power renders the minor incapable of placing some acts validly by himself. His parents or tutors may act for him as his representatives; or the consent or authority of the parents or tutors may be necessary, or in some cases only their assistance and counsel.[8] The reason for

[3] Canon 88, § 1.

[4] Cf. *supra,* Chapter III, note 36.

[5] Cf. Ojetti, *Commentarium in Codicem Iuris Canonici,* II, *Liber Secundus, De Personis* (Romae: Universitas Gregoriana, 1928), p. 14.

[6] Canon 34, § 3, 3°. Cf. Vermeersch-Creusen, *Epitome Iuris Canonici* (3 vols., Mechliniae-Romae: Dessain, 1934-1937), III, n. 120; Piontek, "De Acephalis in Iure Canonico," *Jus Pontificium,* XVII (1937), 73.

In American law an infant becomes of age at the first moment of the day preceding the twenty-first anniversary of his birth, 48 hours, therefore, earlier than in the canonical computation. Cf. Madden, *Handbook on the Law of Persons and Domestic Relations* (St. Paul: West Publishing Co., 1931), p. 527.

[7] Canon 89.

[8] Cf. Michiels, *Principia Generalia de Personis in Ecclesia* (Lublin: Universitas Catholica, 1932), pp. 44-45.

such requirements is to protect the minor's interests as long as he is unable to judge matters soundly and handle his own affairs discreetly. The provision for the tutelage of minors intends also, especially in civil legislation, to protect others who do business with minors.

During his minority a youth enjoys other protections of the law, either civil or ecclesiastical. In the present canon law a minor cannot in most contentious cases be a party to the trial but must be represented by a parent, tutor, or guardian;[9] when the contentious case of a minor does come to court, the judge must appoint an advocate to act as a defender of the minor's interests unless he already has one.[10] Because of these and other manifold devices of the civil laws set up to safeguard the rights and property of minors, *restitutio in integrum* for their sake is not as frequently used as in earlier times.[11] Yet equity prompted its retention in the law for the eventual case wherein a minor is beset with grave damage and bereft of any other remedy with which to repair it adequately In spite of the fact that *restitutio in integrum* is an extraordinary remedy, the minor can invoke it even though he could use an ordinary one as long as *restitutio* is more advantageous to him. As far as minors are concerned, the time-honored adage of civil and ecclesiastical jurisprudence is retained: "To a person having an ordinary remedy, an extraordinary one should not be given, unless it be more advantageous." [12]

If a minor entered a contract through fear, he could invoke an ordinary remedy, a rescissory action, against it.[13] But if it were difficult to prove the existence of fear, the minor could seek *restitutio,* because it would be more advantageous; he would

[9] Canon 1648, § 1.

[10] Canon 1655, § 2. For other situations in which minority is considered by the law, cf. canons 1737, 2352-2354; 2357, 2359, 2204, 2218, 2230.

[11] Roberti, *De Processibus,* I, 389; Wernz-Vidal, *Ius Canonicum,* Vol. VI, *De Processibus* (Romae: Universitas Gregoriana, 1927), n. 316.

[12] Cf. Reiffenstuel, *op. cit.,* I, tit. 41, nn. 4-6; Schmalzgrueber, *op. cit.,* I, tit. 41, n. 3; Coronata, *Institutiones,* III, n. 1215.

[13] Canon 1684, § 1.

have to prove merely his minority and the fact that he was gravely damaged. This is expressed in canon 1687, § 1, regarding minors: *praeter alia ordinaria remedia, suppetit remedium extraordinarium restitutionis in integrum.* Yet the extraordinary remedy cannot be chosen by a minor in preference to an action of nullity if the act is manifestly null. Even the minor must use the action for the declaration of nullity.[14] Canon 1687, § 1, states that *restitutio* is possible *praeter alia ordinaria remedia* to repair damage *ex negotio seu actu valido.* If the act is not valid, the extraordinary remedy is not available. This was equally true in the old law.[15]

The fact that the act in question was either performed with the assistance of a parent or tutor, or carried out by such a one in the minor's name, will not exclude the minor from the benefit of the remedy.[16] This is but equitable; minors are at the mercy of their parents or tutors and may easily suffer from their negligence, ignorance, or malice.[17] But the jurisprudence on the old law excluded minors from seeking *restitutio in integrum* in some circumstances. By virtue of canon 6, n. 2, these exceptions retain their force. If a minor, for example, received permission to act as an adult—*venia aetatis*—he could not later ask for the protection allowed to minors.[18] In the present law at least this *venia aetatis,* or emancipation, would have to come from the civil authorities, since the Church makes few provisions for emancipation from parental power.[19] And in the matter of contracts the civil law is expressly canonized by canon 1529, so that if such a permission is possible in the civil law, it would be

[14] Cf. canons 1679-1680.

[15] Cf. Reiffenstuel, *op. cit.*, I, tit. 41, n. 14, where he cites D. (4, 4) 16, 1-2-3.

[16] Roberti, *De Processibus,* I, 389; Coronata, *Institutiones,* III, n. 1216.

[17] Cf. Woywod, "Rescissory Actions and Restitutio in Integrum,"—*Hom. Past. Rev.,* XXXI (1931), 842.

[18] C. (2, 44) 1. Cf. Coronata, *Institutiones,* III, n. 1216.

[19] Cf., e. g., canons 1648, § 3; 580; Piontek, *Jus Pontificium,* XVII, (1937), 78-79.

recognized in the ecclesiastical forum for the sake of contracts.[20]

Again if an act performed in minority is accepted as binding by the principal after he reaches his majority, *restitutio* will be denied, as that act is considered the deed of an adult.[21] Or if a minor freely swore on oath not to seek this remedy, he could not later repent and invoke it.[22] Or if a minor lied about his age, pretending that he is older than 21 to get someone to do business with him, he should not be helped with this remedy which is intended to assist not the deceiving but the deceived.[23]

The right to seek *restitutio in integrum* passes to the heirs and successors of minors. This quality which the remedy possessed in Roman law [24] has been expressly retained in canon 1687, § 1—*minoribus eorumque heredibus et successoribus.*

Individuals who are above 21 years of age but who because of some defect of body or mind are incapable of managing their own affairs and hence are subject to guardians also come under the protection of minors for the sake of this remedy.[25]

Article II. Persons Assimilated to Minors

In canon law all moral ecclesiastical persons, whether collegiate or non-collegiate, are assimilated to minors [26] and therefore enjoy

[20] Emancipation in American law is effected either by marriage or by act of the parent, but it does not in either case enlarge or effect the infant's capacity to contract; in some States statutes provide for judicial proceedings in courts of chancery or probate which remove the disabilities of infancy. Cf. Madden, *Handbook on the Law of Persons and Domestic Relations*, p. 612.

[21] Cf. Schmalzgrueber, *op. cit.*, I, tit. 41, n. 14. In American law a minor can affirm his acts after reaching majority; cf. Madden, *op. cit.*, pp. 569-572.

[22] Cf. C. 28, X, *de iureiurando*, II, 24; c. 2, *de pactis*, I, 18, in VI°. In the preparatory form of the Code, *Schema E* allowed *restitutio* in spite of an oath to the contrary; this norm, proposed by Many, was omitted—canon 64, Roberti, *Codicis Iuris Canonici Schemata de Processibus*, I, p. 178 and note 9.

[23] Cf. C. (2, 42) 2.

[24] D. (4, 1) 6.

[25] S. R. Rota, *De Manila, legatorum piorum*, 18 febr. 1919—*AAS*, XII (1920), 185.

[26] Canon 100, § 3.

the rights and privileges of minors. This assimilation of corporate entities to minors is an analogy which is to be understood beyond the cases expressly stated in the Code whenever the law grants any favor to minors.[27] The reason is that the moral body, though it be centuries old, is a being whose purely juridical status and character prevent it from acting for itself; it is subject to the management of its administrators just as the minor is to that of his parents or tutor. Like the minor it can therefore suffer grave damage through the negligence or ignorance or even fraud of its temporal administrators.[28]

This privilege of minors found its first statement in the law when Alexander III (1159-1181) proclaimed that the Church enjoyed the rights of minors and therefore the right to *restitutio in integrum* as a minor.[29] It extends not only to the universal Church and to the Holy See, which are moral persons by divine institution, but to all entities erected as moral persons either by law or the concession of a competent ecclesiastical superior[30] It can include, then, an individual church, a diocese, an ecclesiastical province, a religious community either as a unit, as a province or as a single house, a monastery, a cathedral or collegiate chapter, a hospital, orphanage, asylum, a college or university, a benefice. In a word, any collegiate or non-collegiate ecclesiastical moral person coming under the broad terms of canon 100, § 1, is assimilated to a minor in the eyes of the law. It can therefore enjoy the use of *restitutio in integrum* under the wider terms allowed to minors rather than under the restricted conditions specified for adult individuals. Rather than rely, however, on any deduction from the general provision of canon 100, § 3, the legislator makes explicit mention of the ability of moral persons to use *restitutio* as minors in canon 1687, § 1—*minoribus vel minorum iure fruentibus.*

[27] Gillet, *La Personnalité Juridique en Droit Ecclésiastique* (Malines: W. Godenne, 1927), p. 253.

[28] Toso, *Ad Codicem Iuris Canonici . . . Commentaria Minora,* Lib. II, tom. 1 (Citta di Castello: Tipografia Vinciana, 1922), p. 42; Woywod, *Hom. Past. Rev.,* XXXI (1931), 842.

[29] C. 1, X, *de in integrum restitutione,* I, 41.

[30] Canon 100, § 1.

Like minors the moral person needs no special righteous cause for this remedy. For the moral person the cause lies in its inability to protect itself, not because of lack of age but because of its complete reliance on its administrators. All that needs to be demonstrated to the judge is the simple fact that the moral person has suffered grave damage from a valid and rescissible act and that no other equally advantageous remedy is available.[31] The moral person which has validly alienated property for a just price but has thus prejudiced its rights or patrimony can seek *restitutio,* even though it could use an action for the recovery of damages against its administrator in case he had acted negligently or incautiously. *Restitutio,* by rescinding the alienation, restores the moral person to its full stature while the payment of damages may not; and in many cases the administrator would be unable to pay full damages.

It is apparent, then, that for full protection of the moral person this remedy must be open to the successors in the office of the former administrator as well as to that administrator himself.[32] The representative who performed the act may perhaps never realize his folly, or may even refuse to admit that he has compromised his trust. *Restitutio* is conceded not by reason of the person involved but primarily because of the damage suffered.[33] This right of a successor is not due so much to the provision of canon 1687, § 1, which reads *minoribus vel minorum iure fruentibus graviter laesis eorumque heredibus et successoribus* as to the fact that the remedy is given to the moral person. The succeeding administrator is not the successor to the moral person but to his predecessor in office. If, however, the property of one moral person becomes that of another moral person by union or division, the second moral person would be truly the successor to the first and could use *restitutio* because of the clause quoted from canon 1687, § 1.

[31] *Restitutio* could not be chosen in preference to an action for the declaration of nullity of a patently null act, as was noted in connection with minors.

[32] Cf. Schmalzgrueber, *op. cit.,* I, tit. 41, n. 17.

[33] Cf. Lega-Bartoccetti, *op. cit.,* I, 434; Pirhing, *Ius Canonicum,* I, tit. 41, n. 8; Roberti, *De Processibus,* I, 390.

Article III. Adults

By adults are here meant any individual persons who have completed their twenty-first year, the equivalent of the *maiores* in canon 1687, § 2.

The second paragraph of canon 1687 lays down three requirements for the use of *restitutio* by adults over and above the conditions for its use by minors. They are a) that the adult lack any rescissory action or other ordinary remedy; b) that he prove the existence of a special righteous cause for the remedy; and c) that he demonstrate that the damage cannot be imputed to himself.

For adults the adage *"Habenti ordinarium remedium, non est tribuendum extraordinarium"* applies simply and in its severity, without the addition of the qualifying phrase *"nisi hoc sit pinguius."* No matter how much better the extraordinary remedy would repair the damage suffered by an adult, it cannot be employed in his case whenever an ordinary remedy is possible. The canon presupposes the non-availability not only of a rescissory action—the remedy which would be most likely to concur with *restitutio in integrum*—but of any other possible ordinary remedy. *Restitutio* is not excluded if the petitioner is armed with an exception, because this type of defense by which he may retard or defeat the action of another cannot be considered a remedy.[34]

Canon 1687, § 2, further requires that an adult prove the existence of a righteous cause— *dummodo iustam subesse causam probaverint.* The cause which can be a motive for the concession of *restitutio* must be not only the reason for the damage sustained but also an excusing reason for employing this remedy—some impediment which prevented the petitioner from acting in the usual manner and from defending his rights with ordinary remedies.[35] Though great latitude is left to the prudent judge in

[34] Reiffenstuel, *op. cit.,* I, tit. 41, n. 5; Ojetti, however, would deny *restitutio* if an exception existed—*Synopsis Rerum Moralium et Iuris Pontificii* (3. ed., 3 vols., Romae, 1909-1912), n. 3159.

[35] Cf. Pellegrini, *Praxis Vicariorum,* par. II, sect. II, subsect. 11, n. 9; S. R. Rota, *Luganen.,* 16 febr. 1925, dec. XI, n. 3—*Decisiones,* XVII (1925),

determining what constitutes a righteous cause, the judge must be governed in his considerations by the principles of the old law which in this regard remain unchanged by force of canon 6, n. 2.[36] The causes which are accepted by authors and by the jurisprudence of the Rota are chiefly absence, fraud, fear, error, and ignorance; and the general clause of the praetorian edict in Roman law is also included to provide for any other possible righteous cause: *"Item si qua alia mihi iusta causa esse videbitur."* [37]

Before the examination of each of these causes separately it seems advisable to note the third condition laid down by canon 1687, § 2, because of its intimate connection with the righteous cause. An adults must prove also that the damage he suffered is not the result of his own negligence: *et laesionem sibi imputandam non esse probaverint.* This imputability of the damage could inhere either in the malice or in the negligence of the petitioner and the remedy would have to be refused if he were responsible for his own damage because of either. The more frequent occurrence is that of negligence on the part of an adult in not taking precautions to avoid damage and in not making use of the ordinary remedies to repair it. Thus the Rota speaks of a righteous cause that entails damage as one "which excludes *culpa*" and cites the Roman law on the purpose of the remedy: *"Non enim negligentibus subvenitur, sed necessitate rerum impeditis."* [38] An adult would be negligently responsible for the damage he sustained in losing a law-suit during his absence if he foresaw the case and failed to appoint a procurator. The damage is also to be imputed

83; *Incidentis super contumacia,* 24 iulii 1923, dec. XXI, n. 5—*Decisiones,* XV (1923), 183; Lega-Bartoccetti, *op. cit.,* I, 437.

[36] Cf. S. R. Rota, *Luganen.,* 16 febr. 1925, dec. XI, n. 2—*Decisiones,* XVII (1925), 83; Lega-Bartoccetti, *op. cit.,* I, 437; Roberti, *De Processibus,* I, 390.

[37] D. (4, 6) 1, 1. All causes mentioned above are listed by the Rota, *Restitutionis in integrum et diffamationis,* 17 ian. 1923, dec. II, n. 2—*Decisiones,* XV (1923), 12. Cf. also Roberti, *De Processibus,* I, 390; Reiffenstuel, *op. cit.,* I, tit. 41, nn. 13, 51 ff.; Cocchi, *De Processibus,* n. 97.

[38] D. (4, 4) 16. S. R. Rota, *Restitutionis in integrum et diffamatonis,* 17 ian. 1923, dec. II, n. 2—*Decisiones,* XV, (1923), 12.

to the petitioner, even though a just cause like error exists, if he allows the time to lapse in which he could have used an ordinary remedy.[39]

A brief note is now in order on each of the particular causes:

a) Absence. Obviously a person cannot fully defend his property or rights while he is absent from his place of domicile or from the place where his interest lie. From Roman times absence has always been an acceptable cause for the restoration of the status of adults. In Roman law it was chiefly absence for the sake of the republic—the absence of a legate, magistrate, or soldier; but captivity or detention in chains, or flight to avoid the danger of death or some other grave evil was also accepted as a righteous cause.[40] In all these cases one element is common and essential—the absence was somehow necessary rather than voluntary. Such an absence the Rota calls "legitimate."[41] Today any absence that circumstances make necessary is a righteous cause for *restitutio* to repair damage suffered during the absence, while an entirely optional absence usually is not. Even during a necessitated absence damage will be due to negligence if it was foreseen or should have been foreseen and the adult did not appoint a procurator to handle the matter.

Since the law affords other means of protection, *restitutio* because of absence is no longer frequent.[42] The periods of time assigned for the exercise of rights is frequently *usable* time which does not lapse if a person is legitimately impeded;[43] a person necessarily absent is certainly legitimately impeded.

b) Fear. Not only for fear but also for fraud, ignorance, or

[39] Cf. S. R. Rota, *Luganen.*, 16 febr. 1925, dec. XI, n. 2—*Decisiones,* XVII (1925), 83.

[40] Cf. D. (4, 6) 3; 7; 5, 1, 6; 9; 10; 1, 1; C. (2, 53) 1.

[41] *Luganen.*, 16 febr. 1925, dec. XI, n. 2—*Decisiones,* XVII (1925), 83; cf. Roberti, *De Processibus,* I, 390; Wernz-Vidal, *Ius Canonicum,* VI, n. 318.

[42] Cf. Roberti, *De Processibus,* I, 390.

[43] Canon 35. For a list of acts in which *usable* time is allowed, cf. Van Hove, *De Consuetudine De Temporis Supputatione,* Commentarium Lovaniense in Codicem Iuris Canonici, I, tom. III (Mechliniae-Romae: H. Dessain, 1933), n. 319.

error there is a rescissory action in canon law. A minor can choose the extraordinary remedy in preference to the ordinary one if it be more advantageous. The adult can use *restitutio* only in default of an ordinary rescissory action. It is necessary, therefore, to determine to what extent the rescissory actions are available to see what margin remains of these causes as a basis for *restitutio in integrum*.

Fear is a disturbance of mind because of a present or future danger.[44] If the disturbance is such as to render a voluntary act impossible, the act would be null and is to be attacked by an action for the declaration of its nullity.[45] The general principle of canon law, however, is that acts placed through grave and even unjustly aroused fear are valid unless the law provides otherwise, but they can be rescinded.[46] In canon 1684, § 1, a rescissory action is granted for this purpose, to revoke an act placed through grave fear unjustly aroused but not null according to the law. No time limit is placed on this action so that it is extinguished only by being prescribed.[47] Hence an adult would not often be able to invoke *restitutio in integrum* by pleading fear as a righteous cause, since an ordinary remedy is at his disposal. Writers concede that minors could seek *restitutio* because of grave damage if they were unable to prove the existence of fear.[48] There is no reason to restrict this provision to minors. Damage, not fear, is the foundation of *restitutio*. Though the existence of grave fear which was inspired directly to extort consent may not be sufficiently proved and the ordinary action therefore precluded, it may be demonstrated to the judge that grave damage resulted from the act and that the adult would hardly have performed so damaging an act if some fear had not influenced him.

Fear is recognized as a sufficient cause for *restitutio in integrum*

[44] "Instantis vel futuri periculi causa mentis trepidatio"—D. (4, 2) 1.

[45] Cf. canons 1679-1680; Ojetti, *Commentarium*, II, 179.

[46] Canon 103, § 2.

[47] Cf. canons 1701, 1508-1512.

[48] Cf., e. g., Toso, *Commentaria minora*, lib. II, tom. I, p. 51.

by the legislator in canon 103, § 2, which states that acts placed through fear, though not null, can be rescinded *"ad normam can. 1684-1689"*, so as to include the canons on this extraordinary remedy.[49]

Force or external coercion to perform an act, whether it be physical or moral, renders the act null whenever it cannot be resisted.[50] Since it vitiates the act, force cannot be a ground for *restitutio in integrum* in canon law; neither is there a rescissory action because of force. If the force were not sufficient to nullify an act it may be reducible to fear and for this reason the act would be the subject of the rescissory action or of *restitutio.*

c) Fraud. Any "strategy, deceit, device employed to cheat, mislead, deceive another" comes under the term fraud or *dolus.*[51] Canon law places it on a parity with fear in canon 103, § 2, and in canon 1684, § 1, so that what has been said of fear applies also to fraud as a righteous cause for this remedy.

d) Ignorance and error. Although there is a notable difference between ignorance and error, in law they are frequently equivalent in effect.[52] Ignorance is the lack of knowledge that could and should be present; error is a false judgment. Either may concern the law or a fact. Error (or ignorance) either of law or of fact renders an act invalid if it concerns the substance of the

[49] Many authors writing on canon 103 ignore the fact that it refers to *restitutio* as well as to the rescissory actions; cf. Claeys-Bouuaert, "De Metus Influxu quoad valorem actuum, etc.," *Jus Pontificium,* VI (1926), 105-111, especially p. 108; Gillet, "De Actione Rescissoria ob Dolum," *Jus Pontificium,* IX (1929), 323-324. Michiels, however, gives full force to the reference to this remedy in canon 103, § 2—*Principia Generalia de Personis in Ecclesia,* p. 403. Woywod denies the possibility of *restitutio* of adults for fear or fraud or error, or for any reason, in fact, except absence—*Hom. Past. Rev.,* XXXI (1931), 843.

[50] Canon 103, § 1; cf. D. (4. 2) 2.

[51] "Calliditas, fallacia, machinatio ad circumveniendum, fallendum, decipiendum alterum adhibita"— D. (4, 3) 1, 2.

[52] Wernz-Vidal, *Ius Canonicum,* Vol. II, *De Personis* (2. ed., Romae: Universitas Gregoriana, 1928), n. 39; Vermeersch-Cruesen, *Epitome,* I, n. 228.

act or if it is equivalent to a condition *sine qua non.*[53] In such a case *restitutio in integrum* could not be sought. In spite of any other error or ignorance an act is valid unless the law provides otherwise, states canon 104, but in contracts error will allow a rescissory action according to the law. The law referred to is obviously the one regarding a rescissory action in canon 1684, § 2, which allows the revocation of a contract entered in view of a blameless error (i. e. one not provoked by fraud) which results in damage over half the value of the object involved. Error, then, can be the cause for *restitutio* in favor of adults only when it does not nullify the act or when the law does not allow some other remedy for its sake. Outside of contracts, which are the only type of act provided for in canons 104 and 1684, § 1, error or ignorance could cause grave damage for which there would be no ordinary remedy. And even in contracts, canon 1684, § 2, allows the ordinary action only for damage exceeding half the value of the object. The grave damage required for *restitutio in integrum* need not be so large.

The existence of ignorance or error as a ground for rescinding an act by this remedy must usually be proved, because canon 16, § 2, states that ignorance or error is not generally presumed. By stating, however, that it is not generally presumed, the canon seems to imply that ignorance or error is to be presumed in some persons. Thus it is presumed in minors; and most writers on the old law and some on the new presume it also in women, rustics, and soldiers.[54] Since there is no unanimity among recent

[53] Canon 104.

[54] Schmalzgrueber, *op. cit.,* I, tit. 41, n. 9; Pirhing, *Ius Canonicum,* I, tit. 2, n. 54; Romani, "De Ignorantia Legis," *Acta Congressus Iuridici Internationalis* . . . 1934 (5 vols., Romae: Pont. Inst. Utriusque Iuris, 1935-1937), IV, 116-117; *idem, Il Monitore Ecclesiastico,* 5. series, VII (1935), 275. Lega-Bartoccetti (*op. cit.,* I, 437) mentions only women and rustics; Pellegrini (*Praxis Vicariorum,* par. II, sect. II, subsect. 11, n. 19) excludes rustics from a presumption of ignorance and Noval (*De Iudiciis,* n. 344) follows his authority. The Rota in a matrimonial case of 1926 declared that knowledge of the law (without any distinction) is not to be presumed in women—*Southwarcen.,* 29 iulii 1926, dec. XXXV, n. 8—*Decisiones,* XVIII (1926), 286.

writers on whether ignorance is to be presumed in women, rustics, and soldiers, a judge may or may not admit such a presumption in place of proof of the existence of this righteous cause. In any case, a presumption gives way to the truth, and on the judge's admission or rejection of the presumption of ignorance depends the question of whether the petitioner must prove ignorance or whether the defendant must prove the petitioner's knowledge.

Ignorance of the law, it seems, should be more readily admitted than that of fact. The Rota argued once that if a judge can err concerning the law—and the law provides for such a possible case by preparing remedies against the sentence—so much more the parties, especially if they act for themselves in the trial.[55]

e) Any other righteous cause. The Roman praetor made provision in a general clause for any other possible righteous cause for *restitutio in integrum*. So too canon 1687, § 2, merely states that a righteous cause is necessary, leaving its determination to the prudence of the judge. All writers admit that no complete list of the righteous causes for allowing this remedy can be given.[56] Some other causes listed by older writers are sickness, which can easily be considered as equivalent to necessary absence, and immense damage, because damage is the basis of the remedy.[57]

A final question as to *restitutio* in favor of adults is whether the right to seek *restitutio* passes to the heirs and successors of an adult. The phrase *eorumque heredibus et successoribus* appears only in the first paragraph of canon 1687 which concerns minors. In Roman law, however, the heirs of an adult could seek *restitutio*.[58] Commentators on the decretals wrote frequently in a general way as if the right to ask for *restitutio* passed to the

[55] *S. Iacobi de Chile, restitutionis in integrum et compromissi*, 5 iulii 1927, dec. XXXIV, n. 16—*Decisiones*, XIX (1927), 287.

[56] Cf. Romani, *Il Monitore Ecclesiastico*, 5. series, VII (1935), 274-275; Roberti, *De Processibus*, I, 391. Woywod, however, as noted above, admits no cause except absence—*Hom. Past. Rev.*, XXXI (1931), 843.

[57] "laesio enormissima"—Pellegrini, *Praxis Vicariorum*, par. II, sect. II, subsect. 11, n. 9.

[58] D. (4, 1) 6.

heirs and successors of anyone who himself had that right. Yet closer examination reveals that they either treated this question when they were speaking of the *restitutio* of minors or gave examples only of the heirs of minors.[59] It may be concluded, it seems, that canon 1687 restricts the transmissibility of this remedy to the heirs and successors of minors and of those who enjoy the same status. This is not a change in the law but a statement of the canonical jurisprudence which long ago receded from Roman law on this point. Several writers since the Code, by definitely stating that *restitutio* can be sought by heirs and successors of minors, imply that only to these is the right transmitted.[60]

[59] Cf. Schmalzgrueber, *op. cit.,* I, tit. 41, n. 17; Reiffenstuel, *op. cit.,* I, tit. 41, n. 107; Pellegrini, *l. c.,* n. 27.

[60] Wernz-Vidal, *Ius Canonicum,* VI, n. 317; Roberti, *De Processibus,* I, 389; Vermeersch-Cruesen, *Epitome,* III, n. 117.

Chapter VII

THE OBJECT OF THE REMEDY

Canon 1687.—§ 1 . . . ad laesionem reparandam ex negotio seu actu valido rescindibili . . .

Restitutio in integrum can be used to repair the damage rising from any transaction [1] or act which is valid but rescissible. An invalid act cannot be attacked by this remedy because it does not exist in the eyes of the law, and what does not exist cannot be rescinded. The nullity of an act may be due either to the lack of some essential element or to the lack of some solemnity or condition required by the law under sanction of nullity.[2] In many acts and contracts, or agreements of any kind, an essential element is lacking if sufficient consent is not given; force, fear, fraud, or error may prevent the performance of a valid act. In many cases the law demands certain formalities, for example, the consent of a superior or of consultors,[3] without which the act performed is null. In any such case *restitutio* is impossible. If the nullity of the act is not obvious, however, or cannot be proved, then *restitutio in integrum* can be sought subordinately.[4]

In the matter of contracts there is another possibility of nullity. Canon 1529 canonizes the civil law of the region in which the contract is made. If, therefore, a contract is null because of a prescription of the civil law which is not contrary to the divine law or contradicted by the canon law, its nullity is recognized in the ecclesiastical forum. A contract which is null in civil law is to be attacked because of nullity; *restitutio* cannot be granted.[5]

[1] Transaction is here used to translate *negotium* and is not to be confused with the exact sense of *transactio* in canons 1925 ff.

[2] Canon 1680, § 1.

[3] Cf. canons 105, 1530, § 1, 3°.

[4] Noval, *De Iudiciis,* n. 343.

[5] Apparently no writer has made this application of canon 1529 to canon 1687, § 1. Of canon 1529 Vermeersch (*Epitome,* II, n. 850)

Besides being valid an act must be rescissible to be the object of *restitutio*. Rescissible here means only that the act is capable of being rescinded. It does not mean that the act must be weakened by some defect of consent so that it ought in justice to be annulled. All acts vitiated by fear, fraud, or error are the object of rescissory actions. *Restitutio in integrum* is not based on any defect in the act but on the resulting damage.[6] For *restitutio* all that is required is that the damaging act be capable of annulment; the valid contract of marriage or a valid religious profession are therefore excluded. Eichmann excludes also the presentation of a candidate for an office and election to an office.[7] The acts or transactions against which this remedy can be invoked fall most easily into the division of extra-judicial and judicial matters.

Article I. Extra-Judicial Matters

Restitutio in integrum in most extra-judicial matters concerns the defining of property rights. An ecclesiastical judge will intervene to decide concerning temporalities only when by reason of spiritual persons or things he is competent according to canon 1553. When it is stated, therefore, that *restitutio* is possible against contracts or against prescription, it does not follow that in every dispute the church court will accept a petition for *restitutio*. The case must be a spiritual one or at least a temporal one over which the Church claims cognizance because of some spiritual element—a *res mixti fori*.[8] A layman seeking to rescind

says: "Before its meaning and proper strength are certainly known by use and various declarations, many responses of private interpretation must give way to authentic interpretation." Tentatively, therefore, the opinion of the text is stated.

[6] Cf. Coronata, *Institutiones Iuris Canonici*, I (2. ed., Taurini: Marietti, 1939), n. 148; Ferreres, *Institutiones Canonicae iuxta Novissimum Codicem Pii* X (2. ed., 2 vols., Barcelona: Subirana, 1920), II, n. 621; Michiels, *Principia Generalia de Personis*, p. 493; Bernardini, "Problemi di contenzioso amministrativo canonico,"—*Acta Congressus Iuridici Internationalis* . . . 1934, IV, 411, note 29.

[7] *Das Prozessrecht des Codex Iuris Canonici* (Paderborn: Schöningh, 1921), p. 115.

[8] Cf. Ottaviani, *Institutiones Iuris Publici Ecclesiastici*, I, nn. 149-157.

a contract entered into with another layman must go to the civil court for relief; if the civil law does not embrace *restitutio in integrum,* he must attempt other remedies. The church court will not claim competence over such purely civil matters.

Cases of minors were once considered as *res mixti fori,* but since the civil laws now protect minors in many ways, the ecclesiastical court will seldom open the case of a minor for *restitutio* in a purely temporal matter today.[9] There is always the danger, too, that the loser would take the case to the civil court and perhaps have the ruling of the ecclesiastical judge overthrown.

The case of an ecclesiastical moral person seeking this remedy against a layman has long been considered a *res mixti fori,* so that the church court could accept a hearing on it as allowed in the present law by canon 1553, § 2.[10] Again there is of course the danger that in most countries today the vanquished layman could carry his case to the civil court.

Therefore, in discussing cases which define property rights by means of a *restitutio in integrum,* one must understand that reference is made to cases over which the ecclesiastical court claims cognizance. These will be for the greater part cases involving two or more ecclesiastical moral persons. Even in such causes *restitutio* will not be a frequent remedy under the present law.[11] This is due to the precautions taken by canon law to protect the church organizations from grave damage. Contracts entered into by a moral person frequently involve alienation of church property. Alienation, not only in the strict sense of a contract by which the *dominium* of a thing is transferred to another, but even in a wide sense to include any contract or obligation by which the condition of the church would be weakened,[12] is protected by certain solemnities. Most of

[9] Cf. Roberti, *De Processibus,* I, 94.

[10] Cf. Bouix, *De Iudiciis,* II, 418; Coronata, *Institutiones,* III, n. 1090.

[11] Cf. Roberti, *De Processibus,* I, 389.

[12] Cf. canon 1533; Vromant, *De Bonis Ecclesiae Temporalibus* (Louvain: Musseum Lessianum, 1927), n. 279.

these are required only for the licitness of the transaction, but at least the consent of a legitimate superior is necessary for its validity.[13] The statement of such requirements as an estimate of price under which the object is not to be alienated, the existence of a just cause for the contract, even though their neglect will not nullify the transaction, will prevent many contracts from being made which would eventually be attacked by *restitutio in integrum.* Furthermore, if an administrator alienates church property validly but illicitly, a personal action against him is possible.[14] *Restitutio* can be used then only when it is a more advantageous remedy. The non-observance of the civil law solemnities required for the contracts made by corporations would render the alienation civilly invalid and by consequence also canonically invalid by virtue of canon 1529, so that the contract would have to be declared null; it could not then be revoked by *restitutio.*

The general principle remains, however. Given a valid contract, either licit or illicit, *restitutio in integrum* is available to rescind it if the other conditions required by the law are verified. A question rises as to the extent to which canon 1529 embraces the civil law on contracts. Does it canonize the civil law on remedies against a contract, so that if the civil law does not recognize *restitutio* against a contract it is thereby ruled out in the canonical forum? The canon states that "Those prescriptions which the civil law of the territory sets up concerning contracts are to be observed in canon law in ecclesiastical matters with the same effects, unless they be contrary to the divine law or unless the canon law provides otherwise." [15] Though the interpretation of this canon is not as yet entirely clear, the clause "unless the canon law provides otherwise" should not, it seems, be restricted to the canons which follow in the title on contracts,

[13] Canons 1530, § 1, 3°; 1532.

[14] Canon 1524, § 1.

[15] Canon 1529: Quae ius civile in territorio statuit de contractibus tam in genere, quam in specie, sive nominatis sive innominatis, et de solutionibus, eadem iure canonico in materia ecclesiastica iisdem effectibus serventur, nisi iuri divino contraria sint aut aliud iure canonico caveatur.

but refer to the whole law. Canon law does provide otherwise in allowing the extraordinary remedy of *restitutio* against contracts. This remedy can be used, therefore, against a contract in a place where the law of the land does not recognize *restitutio in integrum.* Yet it is obvious how cautiously the remedy must be employed to avoid conflict with the civil law, to avoid having a contract non-existent in the ecclesiastical forum and yet enforceable by civil authority.[16]

It would be useless to attempt to make particular application of *restitutio in integrum* to all the contracts either of the Roman law or of the common law. Writers have always stated that the remedy was possible against all contracts, sometimes giving a list of the more prominent ones.[17] It will be useful to cite a few examples by way of illustration and to note a few exceptions to the general principles on this remedy.

A donation, which is a gratuitous contract, can be revoked by *restitutio.* The law itself provides for the revocation of donations made by prelates and rectors of churches without recourse to the extraordinary remedy if the donations are immoderate and made without an expedient cause like remuneration, piety, or Christian charity.[18] On the other hand, if a donation is illegitimately repudiated by the rector of a church or by the superior of a religious institute, that is, without the permission of the ordinary, the same rector or superior or his successor may be granted a *restitutio in integrum* to accept the donation.[19] This is the only place in the law of the Code on contracts in which special mention is made of this remedy. Even here an action

[16] Vering already in the last century doubted if restoration in favor of the church could be had independently of the civil law. "Can these rules be followed in our days?" he asked, after outlining the law on the remedy. "That depends on the civil legislation of each land."—*Bibliotheque Théologique du XIX Siécle, Droit Canon* (translated by Belet, 2 vols., Paris, 1881), II, 577.

[17] E. g., Schmalzgrueber, *op. cit.*, I, tit. 41, nn. 25 ff.; Bouix, *De Iudiciis,* II, 414.

[18] Canon 1535.

[19] Canon 1536, § 3.

for indemnity is likewise allowed, so that the extraordinary remedy should be granted only when it is more advantageous. The *restitutio* would restore the church or institution to the position it once had of being able to accept the donation. If the prospective donor is no longer willing to make his gift, the restoration is fruitless.[20]

In a contract of sale this extraordinary remedy will not be necessary if the damage results solely from the fact that the price paid was too small; the damage could be repaired by another payment to complete a just price. *Restitutio* will be necessary if the sale of the property should not have taken place; likewise if the seller suffers damage at no matter what price he sold his goods. Then it is a *remedium pinguius* and possible to a minor or one in his juridical position.

Restitutio in integrum can be invoked against a contract of mortagage, loan (*pignus*), or even against a debt which encumbers the whole property of a moral person.[21] In any of these cases, however, when such a contract is rescinded, the debt must be guaranteed in some other manner. *Restitutio* does not allow the party in whose favor it is given to become richer through the rescission of a contract.[22]

Outside of contracts another extra-judicial act which could be attacked by this remedy in the old law was prescription. Thus for four years after the prescription was completed an ecclesiastical moral person could reassert its ownership and have the prescription set aside.[23] This holds true today only if the civil law recognizes the remedy of *restitutio in integrum* against prescription. This is due to the great difference between canon 1508 and canon 1529, which both embrace the civil law. In canon 1529, as has been noted, the civil law on contracts is canonized to the full extent if it is not contrary to the divine

[20] Only the revocation of a legitimately accepted donation to a church is forbidden by canon 1536, § 4.

[21] Vromant, *De Bonis Ecclesiae Temporalibus*, n. 297.

[22] Cf. Lega-Bartoccetti, *op. cit.*, I, 439.

[23] Cf. Schmalzgrueber, *op. cit.*, II, tit. 26, n. 142; Bouix, *De Iudiciis*, II, 413; Noval, *De Iudiciis*, n. 343.

law or if the canon law does not provide otherwise. In canon 1508 the civil law on prescription is likewise canonized as a mode of acquisition or liberation even for ecclesiastical goods, "except for the enactments of the canons which follow." The exception made for canon law in canon 1508 is much narrower than that of canon 1529. It does not extend to the whole Code but only to the canons on prescription, that is, canons 1509 to 1512 inclusive, in which no mention is made of *restitutio in integrum.*[24] Unless, then, the civil law allows it for this purpose, *restitutio* cannot be sought against prescription in the ecclesiastical court.

Article II. Judicial Matters

Restitutio in integrum can also be used in judicial matters, that is, to rescind acts which occur during a formal trial in an ecclesiastical court. Either of the parties to a trial can seek *restitutio* against the judicial act which has gravely damaged his rights, whether the act was placed by himself or by the judge or tribunal. The acts usually noted as constituting possible objects of this extraordinary remedy are the confession of a party; the *fatalia,* or the lapse of time allowed peremptorily for an act, and the judicial sentence. The use of *restitutio* against the sentence is governed by specific regulations in canons 1905-1907.

A confession made in the course of a trial can be revoked by *restitutio in integrum* just as in the old law.[25] A judicial confession is defined in canon 1750 as an "assertion concerning some fact, written or orally given by one party against himself and in favor of his adversary, either spontaneously or in answer to the interrogation of the judge." In a case of private interest which does not concern the public good, such a confession, rightly made, relieves the other party from proving the points covered by the confession.[26] Yet the law, in canon 1751, allows a con-

[24] Cappello states "Hodie, etiam quoad restitutionem, standum est, in foro canonico, legi civili"—"De Praescriptione," *Jus Pontificium,* V. (1925), 22.

[25] C. 2, *de restitutione in integrum,* I, 21, in VI°; cf. Reiffenstuel, *op. cit.,* I, tit. 41, nn. 96 ff.

[26] Canon 1751.

fession to be retracted under certain circumstances; if it is retracted immediately, e. g., before it is written into the acts or in the same session of the court;[27] if it is not made freely and thoughtfully, or if it is due to an error on the part of the author of the confession.[28] Thus several of the righteous causes for the *restitutio* in favor of an adult against his confession are already taken care of by the law—error, fear, or fraud—so that *restitutio in integrum* is not necessary to revoke a confession for these reasons. A minor, granted that he has the right to stand in court, as otherwise his confession would be null,[29] or a moral person could revoke a confession outside of the reasons provided in canon 1752 by receiving a *restitutio in integrum.*[30] Likewise an adult, for some righteous cause not affording retraction of his confession by virtue of canon 1752, could invoke *restitutio;* this follows from the nature of the extraordinary remedy, although most writers pass by such a possibility in silence. *Restitutio* is possible for four years, but if the case is decided and the sentence becomes irrevocably adjudged, the sentence can be attacked only on the grounds allowed by canon 1905.[31]

Lega considers *restitutio* possible to quash a citation.[32] Though it is difficult to conceive a situation in which the citation alone would be the cause of grave damage, the possibility is not to be denied.

Restitutio in integrum is also useful to remove the effects of a decree declaring one of the parties to be in contempt of court. In the new law a party can be declared contumacious only for not appearing in court when properly summoned or for failing

[27] Coronata, *Institutiones,* III, n. 1278.

[28] Cf. canon 1752.

[29] Cf. canons 1642, 1892, 2°; Roberti, *De Processibus,* II, 34.

[30] Coronata, *Institutiones,* III, n. 1277; Lega-Bartoccetti, *op. cit.,* I, 438.

[31] Cf. Coronata, *Institutiones,* III, n. 1278; Muniz, *Procedimientos Eclesiásticos* (2 ed., 3 vols., Sevilla: Sobrino de Izquierdo, 1926), III, n. 292.

[32] Lega-Bartoccetti, *op. cit.,* I, 436.

to give an excuse for his absence.[33] Once a party has been declared to be in contempt of court the trial can proceed even to a decision in a definitive sentence.[34] If the contumacious party decides to come into court before the sentence is pronounced, he must ordinarily accept the case as it stands; even then he may present proofs and his conclusions, if it is not too late for them.[35] But the acts which have taken place prior to his appearance will not be repeated for his benefit, unless he receives a *restitutio in integrum* which wipes out the effects of his contempt. To receive the remedy it will be necessary for the adult to have a righteous cause which will almost necessarily be that he never received the citation or that he was impeded from appearing or that he was ignorant of the law. Any of these reasons would amount to clearing himself of contempt. Roberti [36] requires that the party clear himself of contempt to receive *restitutio in integrum* during the trial. Hanssen [37] says that it can be validly given even though he remain contumacious, because of the nature of the remedy. This is quite true, but it is difficult to imagine a righteous cause for *restitutio* which would not at the same time clear the party of contempt. A moral person or a minor would not of course need a specific righteous cause for *restitutio* and therefore would not need to clear himself of contempt.

This *restitutio* is not to be confused with that granted by canon 1847 to a contumacious party to appeal from the definitive sentence; consideration of canon 1847 will be better postponed to the treatment of *restitutio* as a remedy against the sentence.

[33] Canons 1842-1843; 1848. For a clear comparison of the old and new law on contumacy, cf. S. R. Rota, *Incidentis super contumacia,* 24 iulii 1923, dec. XXI, nn. 8-10—*Decisiones,* XV (1923), 185-187; D'Ambrosio, "De contumacia iudiciali in antiqua et nova iuris can. disciplina," *Jus Pontificium,* IV (1924), 11-20.

[34] Canon 1844.

[35] Canon 1846. Cf. Roberti, *De Processibus,* II, 134; Coronata, *Institutiones,* III, 1377.

[36] *De Processibus,* II, 135; likewise Connolly, *Appeals,* The Catholic University of America Canon Law Studies, n. 79, (Washington: Catholic University of America, 1932), p. 84.

[37] "De Sanctione nullitatis in processu canonico," *Apollinaris,* XI (1938), 400.

In the old law another use of *restitutio* was that against the lapse of time allowed to perform an act—to present proof, to make an exception, to appeal, etc. Since the lapse of the ten days allowed for an appeal results in the sentence becoming irrevocably adjudged,[38] a discussion of this question of restoration against the lapse of the *fatalia appellationis* belongs to the commentary on canons 1905-1907. The same is true of restoration against any lapse of time which results in the sentence becoming irrevocably adjudged; such are the month allowed to begin prosecution of an appeal and the year allowed to complete an appeal case.[39]

The present law does not set up *fatalia* for the presentation of proof. The judge is to determine the time allowed for preparing proofs and procuring witnesses; he can likewise allow more time for a just cause.[40] *Restitutio in integrum* against such a lapse of time, though possible, will not often be necessary under the present law.[41]

[38] Canon 1902, 2°.

[39] Cf. Canons 1883, 1736.

[40] Canon 1634, § 2.

[41] Cf. Pirhing, *Ius Canonicum,* I, tit. 41, n. 22; Leurenius, *Forum Ecclesiasticum,* I, tit. 41, q. 1072; Reiffenstuel, *op. cit.,* I, tit. 41, nn. 80-81.

CHAPTER VIII

THE REMEDY AT WORK

Two canons exhaust the remaining questions on *restitutio in integrum* and describe the remedy at work. The time limit for seeking it and the competent judge are set down in canon 1688; the effects of the remedy are delineated in canon 1689; the procedure in court to discuss a petition for *restitutio* simply follows the general procedural norms.

ARTICLE I. TIME LIMIT

Canon 1688.—§ 1. Restitutio in integrum peti debet . . . intra quadriennium ab adepta maioritate computandum, si agatur de minoribus, a die laesionis et cessati impedimenti, si de maioribus aut personis moralibus.

Restitutio in integrum is to be sought within four years. Because it is an extraordinary remedy granted on grounds of equity rather than of strict justice, the time in which it can be sought is limited by the law while most ordinary actions are extinguished only by prescription.[1] Especially since *restitutio* tends to set aside acts recognized as binding before the law, it is expedient that the possible time for its use be curtailed; it is contrary to the social well-being to allow the final value of juridical affairs to remain uncertain.[2] In classical Roman law *restitutio* was possible within a year. Justinian extended the period to a *quadriennium continuum,* which was taken over into canon law.[3]

In determining the beginning of this four year period again a distinction is made by the canon between minors and adults; here moral persons are grouped not with minors but with adults

[1] Cf. canon 1701. The law sets limits for some actions; cf. canons 1684, § 2; 1893; Lega-Bartoccetti, *op. cit.,* I, 436.

[2] Cf. "La Restituzione in Intero," *Il Monitore Ecclesiastico,* 5. series. VII (1935), 275.

[3] C. (2, 52) 7; c. 1, *de restitutione in integrum,* I, 21, in VI°.

for the obvious reason that they never become of age so that the time cannot be computed from the date of their majority. Since the inability of a moral person is not due to a lack of maturity, the period of grace for seeking the remedy can begin immediately with the damaging act.

From the canon it is apparent that in the case of moral persons and adults the time is to be considered *usable time* at least at the point of its beginning; that is, the time does not begin to lapse from the day on which the damaging act occurs if the person should be legitimately impeded from seeking the remedy. Such is the force of the phrase *et cessati impedimenti.* One could argue from canon 1688, § 1, that the period of four years should be computed as *usable time* only at the point of its beginning but as *continuous time* throughout its course relative to adults and moral persons, and that with reference to minors it should be considered simply as *continuous* from the day they reach majority. The phrase *et cessati impedimenti* seems to be limited to the provision for the beginning of the course of time for adults and moral persons.[4] Furthermore, of its very nature time is continuous and any period should therefore be presumed as *continuous time* unless the law provides to the contrary.

The law, however, may allow the period to be computed as usable time either explicitly or implicitly.[5] And recent writers almost unanimously consider the quadriennium of canon 1688, § 1, as *usable time* in the fullest sense and for all petitioners.[6] This is true by virtue of the old law which considered the quadriennium as a period of *usable time*[7] and which is still in force according to the principles of canon 6, n. 2. Roberti feels that the reason for this quadriennium being conceded in the

[4] This is Augustine's interpretation of the canon—*A Commentary on Canon Law,* VII, 137-138.

[5] Cf. Van Hove, *De Consuetudine De Temporis Supputatione,* n. 319.

[6] Cf. canon 35; cf. Roberti, *De Processibus,* I, 392; Wernz-Vidal, *Ius Canonicum,* VI, n. 320; Muniz, *Procedimientos Eclesiásticos,* III, n. 74; Vermeersch-Cruesen, *Epitome,* III, n. 120; Van Hove, *loc. cit.;* Cocchi, *De Processibus,* III, n. 98; Coronata, *Institutiones,* III, n. 1217.

[7] Cf. e. g., Rieffenstuel, *op. cit.,* I, tit. 41, nn. 59-65.

character of usable time is to render unnecessary any prohibition of granting a *restitutio in integrum* against the lapse of the four year period allowed for this same remedy. Such a prohibition was explicit in the old law.[8]

As usable time, then, the quadriennium for minors can begin with the first moment of the day following upon their twenty-first birthday. The natural impediment of age ceases then. If by some hindrance they are impeded from acting, their condition becomes the same as that of adults. For moral persons and adults the four year period begins to lapse from the time when the damaging act occurred if no impediment stands in the way. The day itself on which the damaging act occurred would not be counted because the "day from which" is not computed in usable time; the *terminus a quo* is alway implicitly determined in the law but it does not necessarily coincide with the beginning of the day.[9]

If minors were impeded from seeking the remedy at the time when they reached their majority, or if moral persons and adults were under a hindrance on the day of the harmful act, then the four year period of usable time would begin to run its course with the beginning of the day which follows upon the cessation of the impediment. The four years are then to be computed in calendar fashion if no new impediment intervenes, and their lapse would be complete with the fourth annual recurrence of the same date.[10] If the parties were not hindered from seeking the remedy at the time of majority or of the damaging act but later became impeded, by sickness for instance, then the continued lapse of time would be interrupted. With such intermissions the year is to be computed as consisting of 365 days on

[8] C. un., *de restitutione in integrum,* I, 11, in Clem.; cf. Roberti, *De Processibus,* I, 392; Coronata, *Institutiones,* III, n. 1217.

[9] Canon 34, § 3, 3°; cf. Van Hove, *De Consuetudine De Temporis Supputatione,* nn. 320-321; Vermeersch-Creusen, *Epitome,* III, n. 120. If, however, the damaging act did coincide with the beginning of a day there is no reason why that day should not be computed; cf. canon 34, § 3, 2°.

[10] Cf. canon 34, § 3, 1°.

which the proper opportunity was offered for seeking the remedy.[11]

In the old law it was necessary that the discussion of a case for *restitutio in integrum* be finished within the four years; now canon 1688, § 1, requires only that the petition be made in that time. Like any other case before a court of first instance it should, according to canon 1620, be finished within two years of its inception.[12]

The heirs and successors of persons, physical or moral, to whom the right to ask for *restitutio* has been transmitted, have only as much time as the principal would have had, granted that they are aware of their right and are not impeded. Thus, if a person who had entered a damaging contract as a minor died at twenty-three, his heirs would have two years in which to seek the remedy.[13]

Article II. The Competent Judge

Canon 1688.—§ 1. Restitutio in integrum peti debet ab ordinario iudice, qui competens est respectu illius, contra quem petitur. . .

Two points concerning the judge who can grant *restitutio in integrum* are settled by the first paragraph of canon 1688: first, that he must be an "ordinary judge," and second, that he must be one "who is competent with respect to him against whom the remedy is sought."

Restitutio is to be sought from an ordinary judge, that is, one having judicial power in virtue of his office,[14] and not from one who has delegated power to judge a particular case. In Roman law *restitutio* could be granted only by the praetor or

[11] Cf. canon 34, § 2.

[12] If no processual act is placed in this time, the case abates—canon 1736; cf. Wernz-Vidal, *Ius Canonicum*, VI, n. 320. For a case before the Rota in which it was declared that a suit for *restitutio* had abated for this reason, cf. *AAS*, XX (1928), 56.

[13] Cf. Coronata, *Institutiones*, III, n. 1216; Wernz-Vidal, *Ius Canonicum*, VI, n. 320.

[14] Cf. canons 197, § 1; 1573, § 1.

the provincial governor, for these judges enjoyed not only jurisdiction but also *imperium,* which was an administrative power. In decretal law the power to grant this remedy was limited to "ordinary judges having administration." [15] The present law in canon 1688 limits the power of granting *restitutio* to "ordinary" judges, to the exclusion of delegated ones. Besides the Roman Pontiff for the universal Church, the Bishop is the ordinary judge in his diocese; [16] likewise the Official has ordinary power and constitutes one tribunal with the bishop.[17] And the Vice-Official, when he acts in the place of the Official, is an ordinary judge, for the power is inherent in the office.[18]

The word "ordinary" in the canon excludes delegated judges from this power because "ordinary" is the common antithesis of "delegated" in the law.[19] A delegated judge can grant this remedy if the power to do so has been specifically delegated to him,[20] or if the question arises incidentally in a case before him, because delegated power always carries with it the authority to decide incidental cases.[21] A delegated judge could be called upon to grant a *restitutio* against the lapse of time he had granted for the presentation of proof, against his own decree of contumacy, etc.

In the old law arbiters could not grant this remedy.[22] In the new law it is also clear that arbiters and arbitrators cannot grant

[15] C. 9, X, *de in integrum restitutione,* I, 41; cf. Bouix, *De Iudiciis,* II, 416.

[16] Canon 1572, § 1.

[17] Canon 1573, § 1.

[18] Cf. canon 1573, § 3; Roberti, *De Processibus,* I, 165.

[19] Cf. canons 197 ff.

[20] Cf. canon 199, § 1.

[21] Canon 200, § 1: ". . . cui tamen delegata potestas est, ea quoque intelliguntur concessa, sine quibus eadem exerceri non posset." Cf. Roberti, *De Processibus,* I, 392. It is needless, therefore, to invoke canon 6, n. 2, to retain this provision of c. 9, X, *de in integrum restitutione,* I, 41, as do Noval (*De Iudiciis,* n. 345) and Blat (*Commentarium Textus Codicis Iuris Canonici, Lib. IV De Processibus* [Romae: Collegio Angelico, 1927], n. 175).

[22] C. 9, X, *de in integrum restitutione,* I, 41.

restitutio, since they do not enjoy ordinary judicial power.[23] And though the Rota is an ordinary tribunal, it is one of appeal and not usually one of the first instance;[24] but petitions for *restitutio in integrum* against any act save the judicial sentence must be presented to a court of the first instance so that the Rota will not be competent to receive them. It could of course grant a *restitutio* in an incidental question rising in a case on trial; but as a principal case it would receive a petition for it only in cases instituted against persons whose trial is reserved to the tribunals of the Holy See or in cases which the Roman Pontiff commits to the Rota.[25] Over *restitutio in integrum* against the judicial sentence which has become irrevocably adjudged the competence of the Rota and of the Signatura will be noted later.

To grant this remedy an ordinary judge must moreover "be competent with respect to him against whom it is sought." This is an application of the principle *"Actor sequitur forum rei."*[26] This does not limit the competency of a judge over the *pars conventa* to that competency which rises from domicile or quasi-domicile.[27] A judge may be competent over the party against whom the remedy is sought by any of the grounds for competency considered in Section I, Title I, *De Foro Competenti,* of the Fourth Book of the Code. Some cases would be limited to the Roman Pontiff or to the tribunals of the Apostolic See;[28] others would have a necessary forum by reason of canon 1560; others a voluntary forum in the place where the object involved is located[29] or in the place where the contract in question was made, or is to be fulfilled, or in the place where the parties to the contract agreed to settle litigation arising from it.[30] If there are several courts competent with respect to the person

[23] Cf. canons 1929, 1932.
[24] Canon 1598, § 1.
[25] Canon 1599, § 2.
[26] Canon 1559, § 3.
[27] Cf. canons 1561-1563.
[28] Canon 1577.
[29] Canon 1564.
[30] Canon 1565.

against whom the remedy is asked, the choice lies with the petitioner.[31]

ARTICLE III. RESTITUTIO GRANTED "EX OFFICIO"

Canon 1688.—§ 2. Minoribus vel minorum iure fruentibus restitutio concedi potest a iudice etiam ex officio, audito vel instante promotore iustitiae.

Restitutio in integrum in favor of adults can be granted only on the petition of the party concerned because it is a concession in the interest of a private party and not for the common good.[32] Minors and moral persons can bring in a petition for this remedy themselves and usually they must do so because otherwise the existence of a damaging act will not be known to the court. A minor may even before his majority call his plight to the attention of the court. The judge should then provide him with a defender or procurator and hear the case.[33]

The judge may also grant *restitutio in integrum* for the sake of a minor or of a moral person enjoying the rights of a minor without the presentation of a petition by the party. This is an exercise of the "noble office" of the judge,[34] and is termed an *ex officio* concession of the remedy by canon 1688, § 2.[35] If a judge observes that a minor or an ecclesiastical moral person has suffered grave damage from some act or transaction, he can commence a hearing to grant *restitutio*. Likewise the promoter of justice if he should notice such a state of affairs, should ask the judge to grant the remedy. This *ex officio* concession of the remedy is allowed to minors, but not to persons who have already attained their majority, even if the damaging act occurred during their minority; such persons must enter a

[31] Canon 1599, § 3.

[32] Cf. canon 1618.

[33] Canon 1655, § 2.

[34] Cf. Coronata, *Institutiones,* III, nn. 1147, 1217.

[35] The term *ex officio* is used in distinction to *ad instantiam partis* so that any concession of this remedy without the presentation of a libellus by the interested party is *ex officio,* whether the judge acts on his own initiative on at the instance of the promoter of justice; cf. Blat, *De Processibus,* n. 175.

pertition as adults.[36] The most frequent case in which the remedy will be granted *ex officio* will be that in favor of ecclesiastical moral persons over which the promoter of justice as the protector of the common good should keep a watchful eye.[37]

The present canon merely states that in line with his public office the judge *can* grant the extraordinary remedy to minors and to moral persons. But what the law thus makes possible the law also seems to inculcate as a possible duty. The duty to bring to a hearing any such case as comes to his attention could rest not only with the judge but also with the promoter of justice whenever a minor or a moral person needlessly suffered damage.[38]

Whenever the judge, either because of his own observation or because of the advice of the promoter of justice, decides to hear the arguments for the remedy *ex officio,* the presence of the promoter is necessary. If the judge himself feels that *restitutio* is advisable against some damaging act, then the promoter must be cited and given an opportunity to offer his consultation in the case—*audito promotore iustitiae*—as canon 1688, § 2, requires. This is necessary for the validity of the acts of the case. According to canon 1587, in any cause in which the presence of the promoter of justice is demanded by law, the acts of the case will be null if he is not cited, unless, even without being cited, he was nevertheless present for at least some of the acts so that he could review the case in order to make his recommendations concerning it. If it is the promoter who deems the remedy advisable for a particular minor or moral person, he will press the case with the judge—*instante promotore iustitiae.* His presence would again be necessary for the validity of the acts of the case.

[36] Augustine (*A Commentary on Canon Law,* VII, 138) says that religious are comparable to minors in the law, so that also in their favor this remedy could be granted *ex officio;* he does not indicate any legal source or doctrine on which he bases this opinion which assimilates religious to minors.

[37] Cf. canon 1586.

[38] Cf. Glynn, *The Promoter of Justice,* The Catholic University of America Canon Law Studies, n. 101, (Washington: Catholic University, 1936), p. 212; Noval, *De Iudiciis,* n. 345.

Article IV. Procedure

Since no particular norms for procedure in granting *restitutio in integrum* are set down in the Code, the general rules of procedure are to be followed.[39]

If the petition for the remedy is entered as an incidental question, e. g., if it is asked during a trial to retract a confession, the petition is to be treated as any other incidental question and settled according to canon 1840. The judge is to decide if it is to be defined by a decree or if full judicial form is to be observed because of the quality and gravity of the question.[40]

In any case in which the *restitutio* is the principal issue, for example, when the petition seeks the rescission of a contract, the question requires a judicial trial like any ordinary action. Although *restitutio* is not strictly an *actio,* the hearing for its concession is a judicial process and the law nowhere exempts the judge from observing the ordinary norms of procedure. An introductory libellus is to be presented, the other party cited and heard;[41] the issue is to be joined[42] and proofs accepted and adjudged according to the general norms of Book IV, Part I. In the case of an adult requesting to be restored to his previous condition, several things must be proved in the trial which are not required in the case of a minor or moral person: the adult must prove the existence of a righteous cause, that the damage is not to be imputed to him, that no ordinary remedy is available.[43]

A procurator needs a special mandate to seek *restitutio* as a principal cause. In an incidental question he does not need one. This is and has been the common opinion of authors on the new and old law, but canon law itself has never clearly stated such

[39] Cf. Lega-Bartoccetti, *op. cit.,* I, 436.

[40] Lega-Bartoccetti, *loc. cit.*

[41] Reiffenstuel, *op. cit.,* I, tit. 41, nn. 16-20; Coronata, *Institutiones,* III, n. 1217.

[42] Cf. c. 2, X, *de officio iudicis,* I, 32; c. 2, X, *ut lite non contestata non procedatur ad testium receptionem vel ad sententiam definitivam,* II, 6; Panormitanus, *Commentaria,* I, *de officio iudicis,* c. 2, n. 7.

[43] Canon 1687, § 2.

a requirement although the Roman law did.[44] Honorius III (1216-1227), in a decretal granting a *restitutio in integrum,* noted that the procurator of the Archbishop of Braga exhibited a special mandate to seek the remedy.[45] The Pontiff may have merely narrated a fact without implying any obligation,[46] but the Gloss on the text read into it the necessity of a mandate on the part of the procurator.[47] Authors have since deemed it a requirement.[48] The Code indeed, in canon 1662, lists certain acts for which a procurator needs a special mandate and adds that one is necessary "in general to do those things for which the law requires a special mandate." That the law requires a special mandate for *restitutio in integrum* is the constant tenet of jurisprudence founded on the Gloss and on Roman law.

Should the promoter of justice be called in for every hearing on this remedy in favor of a minor or ecclesiastical moral person? Canon 1688, § 2, clearly requires his presence if the remedy is to be conceded to one of these parties *ex officio.* What if it is sought by minors or moral persons on their own petition? It is certainly desirable that the promoter of justice be called upon to act in his official capacity and protect the common good by aiding those who cannot defend their own rights. Yet the law does not warrant the stand, taken by Glynn, that the promoter's presence is required in such a case under sanction of the nullity of the proceedings.

In his commentary of canon 1586, which gives a broad outline of the promoter's duties, Glynn admits that it cannot be argued from that canon "that the absence of the promoter would invali-

[44] D. (4, 4) 25, 1.

[45] C. 7, X, *de in integrum restitutione,* I, 41.

[46] Cf. Pirhing, *Ius Canonicum,* I, tit. 41, n. 22, note 2.

[47] Cf. Panormitanus: "Nota tu canonista textum, iuncta glossa, quia non habes alibi in corpore iuris canonici, quod ad petendam restitutionem in integrum, requiritur speciale mandatum,"—*Commentaria,* I, *h. t.,* c. 7, n. 4.

[48] Cf. Pirhing, *loc. cit.;* Covarruvias, *Variorum Resolutionum,* I, c. VI, n. 1; Reiffenstuel, *op. cit.,* I, tit. 38, nn. 103-104; Schmalzgrueber, *op. cit.,* I, tit. 38, n. 27; Roberti, *De Processibus,* I, 331; Hanssen, "De sanctione nullitatis in processu canonico,"—*Apollinaris,* XI (1938), 262.

date" the proceedings in all of the cases in which Glynn deems his presence advisable.[49] Yet when he treats the particular case of *restitutio* for a minor or moral person upon the petition of the party, he states without hesitation that the complete absence of the promoter would invalidate the acts of the case and therefore the sentence or decree. He bases this conclusion apparently on canon 1688, § 2, together with canons 105, n. 1, and 1587, § 1.[50] But canon 1688, §2, refers only to the concession of the remedy *ex officio*. Canon 105, n. 1, states the general principle that whenever the law requires that another's opinion be heard before acting, it is enough for the validity of the act that such an opinion be heard, even though it be disregarded; and the only case in which the law on *restitutio* requires the promoter to be heard is in canon 1688, § 2, when the remedy is being granted on the initiative of the court. Finally, canon 1587, § 1, sets up the sanction of nullity for the proceedings in which the promoter is entirely ignored in causes for which his presence is required; but his presence is not required in the canons on *restitutio*. Nor is the general statement of canon 1586 that the Promoter is constituted "for contentious causes in which the public good, in the judgment of the Ordinary, can be brought into danger," sufficient to conclude that his presence is required for cases of *restitutio* which are not heard *ex officio* unless the Ordinary decides he should be cited. The requirement of his presence by the law is to be known, as Blat points out, through the canons on the individual cases.[51]

If a petition for *restitutio in integrum* is once denied, it can-

[49] *The Promoter of Justice,* p. 90. He gives a demonstrative list of cases involving the public good, including cases of minors and moral persons in general.

[50] These are the three canons cited in note 38 appended to his argument—*ibid.,* p. 212.

[51] ". . . in quibus eorum . . . ad iuris normam cognoscendam per canones de illis causis conditos praesentia equidem activa requiritur iure"—*De Processibus,* n. 47. If the ordinary decrees that the presence of the promoter is necessary in an individual case, then that official must be cited or at least present without citation for the validity of the acts of the cause; cf. Glynn, *op. cit.,* p. 92.

not be sought again and conceded.[52] But a sentence refusing the remedy may be attacked by all possible remedies against a sentence—appeal, the plaint of nullity, or even *restitutio*. When the extraordinary remedy is sought against a sentence or decree which denied a previous petition for *restitutio in integrum*, an entirely new case arises. As a remedy against the sentence it is regulated by canons 1905-1907.

ARTICLE V. EFFECTS

Canon 1689. Restitutio in integrum id efficit ut omnia revocentur in pristinum, idest restituantur in statum quo erant ante laesionem, salvis iuribus quae alii, bona fide, ante petitam restitutionem quaesiverint.

The general effect of *restitutio in integrum* which has been granted by a competent judge is the same regardless of what the object of the remedy may be or in whose favor it may be granted. It is, says canon 1689, to return all things to their original state, that is, to the state in which they were before the damaging act occurred. All things—*omnia*—are restored to their previous condition. Hence both parties, the petitioner and the party against whom the remedy is granted, are to be restored; neither should become richer or poorer, neither should be at greater or less advantage than he was before the act which is now rescinded took place.

With this general principle in mind it is but necessary to examine each type of act or transaction against which *restitutio* can be employed to see how it applies. If a sale is rescinded, the object sold is returned to the seller and the price to the buyer; if a restoration is given against the lapse of time, just so much time is gained once more, e. g., two weeks to present documentary proofs; if a *transactio* is quashed, both parties stand with the same rights they held before transacting; if *restitutio* restores the right to accept an inheritance which had been repudiated, the inheritance returns to the petitioner with all its rights and obliga-

[52] C. 10, X, *de in integrum restitutione,* I, 41; cf. Reiffenstuel, *op. cit.,* I, tit. 41, nn. 39-40; Coronata, *Institutiones,* III, n. 1217.

tions; if a compromise effected by arbitration is rescinded, the parties are free to seek a new means of settlement.

In the individual case difficulties will frequently arise for the judge who must effect this return to the previous condition. A mere return of an object sold on the one side and of the price paid on the other will not be sufficient if the object has deteriorated. The judge must provide for indemnifying the party who receives back his property in a worse condition.[53] On the other hand, if the buyer has improved the property in any necessary or useful way, he must be repaid for his expenses or labor.[54]

The question of the fruits of the thing which is being restored is also a vexing one for the judge. The general rule that "the accessory follows the principal" is to be applied with exceptions and distinctions on which the writers are commonly in accord. In a gratuitous contract—e. g., in the rescission of a donation—the fruits are to be restored with the principal thing because the person restoring suffers no harm and loses nothing that was his own prior to the contract; expenses should, however, be deducted.[55]

In an onerous contract a distinction is made between fruits acquired by the one party before the other made his petition for *restitutio in integrum* and those acquired afterwards. The petition for the remedy is considered to destroy good faith, so that all fruits received after the petition is entered should be restored. If the fruits acquired before the petition have been legally prescribed with a title and good faith, there is no reason for their restoration. Nor is restitution to be made for those fruits acquired too recently to be possessed by legal prescription but which have already been consumed. The unconsumed fruits

[53] Cf. Woywod, *Hom. Past. Rev.,* XXXI (1931), 844-845.

[54] Cf. c. 1, X, *de in integrum restitutione,* I, 41; Wernz-Vidal, *Ius Canonicum,* VI, n. 321; Cocchi, *De Processibus,* n. 99.

[55] Cf. Reiffenstuel, *op. cit.,* I, tit. 41, n. 130; Santi, *Praelectiones Iuris Canonici* (2 vols., Ratisbonae, 1886), I, tit. 41, n. 16; De Angelis, *Praelectiones Iuris Canonici ad methodum Decretalium Gregorii IX exactae* (4 vols., Romae, 1877-1887), I, tit. 41, n. 6; Vromant, *De Bonis Ecclesiae Temporalibus,* n. 301; Noval, *De Iudiciis,* n. 346.

acquired before the petition for *restitutio in integrum* and not yet prescribed should ordinarily be restored; but if the other party does not demand them, they could be kept with good conscience.[56] In applying these principles the Rota once ordered that all fruits acquired prior to the petition for *restitutio in integrum* which were not prescribed and not consumed should be restored to the petitioner. But in another hearing of the case the *turnus* held that there was no need to restore the unconsumed fruits; the reason given was that the authors were not unanimous as to this obligation; though more probably such fruits should be restored, in case of doubt the condition of the possessor is the better.[57]

It is to be noted that these rules are one-sided, contemplating a case in which only one party is bound to the restoration of fruits. The case just cited from the Rota was of this kind. In an onerous contract, however, fruits may have been acquired on both sides. In such a situation some writers allow the fruits of the one to compensate for the fruits of the other. For example, in the case of the sale of a farm, the interest on the price received could compensate for the produce of the farm or the rent from it.[58] The principles previously noted from Reiffenstuel can, however, be adapted to the double restitution of fruits which would be necessary when fruits have accrued to both parties.

So much for the effects of a concession of *restitutio* on the two original parties concerned. The latter part of canon 1689 makes a notable innovation in the law with regard to a third party. It states the exception: "saving the rights which others have acquired in good faith before the petition for *restitutio* is made." Because of the plural verb, *quaesiverint,* the word *alii*

[56] Cf. Reiffenstuel, *op. cit.,* I, tit. 41, nn. 131-135; Vromant, *loc. cit.;* Coronata, *Institutiones,* III, n. 1218; Lega-Bartoccetti, *op. cit.,* I, 439; Wernz-Vidal, *Ius Canonicum,* VI n. 321; Noval, *loc. cit.*

[57] *De Manila, legatorum piorum,* 7 febr. 1916— *AAS,* VIII (1916), 286; *idem,* 18 febr. 1919—*AAS,* XII (1920), 200. "In pari . . . causa, potior est conditio possidentis."—Reg. 65, R. J. in VI°.

[58] Santi, *Praelectiones,* I, tit. 41, n. 16; De Angelis, *Praelectiones,* I, tit. 41, n. 6.

obviously refers to third parties, not to the party against whom the remedy is given. The exception is general—*salvis iuribus*—so that it includes even the right to possession of the object. Thus *restitutio in integrum* is impossible to the extent of restoring the original object which has changed hands, if the new owner acquired his possession in good faith. Some writers seem unaware of the extent of this exception in the new law, as Roberti remarks,[59] since they apply the last half of canon 1689 only to fruits acquired by a third party, implying that the third party would be required to restore the object itself if he had gained possession of it in good faith.[60] On the contrary, if a third party had acquired the object in good faith, the petitioner must take refuge in an action for indemnity against the original party to the transaction.[61]

[59] *De Processibus,* I, 393.

[60] Thus Noval, *De Processibus,* n. 346. Roberti *(loc. cit.)* also ascribes this fault to Vermeersch-Cruesen, but in the fifth edition of the *Epitome* (III, n. 121) the question is ignored. Rightly, Woywod, *Hom. Past. Rev.,* XXXI (1931) 845; Cocchi, *De Processibus,* n. 99; Cappello, *Summa Iuris Canonici* (3 vols., Romae: Universitas Gregoriana, 1936-1939), III, n. 191.

[61] Cf. Woywod, *Hom. Past. Rev.,* XXXI, (1931), 845.

SECTION B. THE REMEDY AGAINST THE SENTENCE

Chapter IX

CONDITIONS FOR USE AGAINST THE SENTENCE

In the old law the judicial sentence was one of the objects of the general remedy of *restitutio in integrum.* In the new law this use of *restitutio* has been separated from the general treatment on actions and placed in that section of the law which deals with the remedies against the sentence. New and stringent conditions are enacted for its use in canon 1905; specific rules for the competence of the judge are set up in canon 1906; particular effects are noted in canon 1907. *Restitutio in integrum* as a remedy against the sentence is now practically a different remedy from that against other acts.

The discussion of the remedy against the sentence will be absolved in three chapters: the present chapter will delineate the conditions of canon 1905 in general; the next will be devoted to the disputed interpretation of canon 1905, § 2, 4°; the last will include the legislation of canon 1906 on the remedy's effects.

Canon 1905.—§ 1. Adversus sententiam contra quam non suppetat ordinarium remedium appellationis aut querelae nullitatis, datur remedium extraordinarium restitutionis in integrum intra fines can. 1687, 1688, dummodo de evidenti iniustitia rei iudicatae manifesto constet.

§ 2. De iniustitia autem manifesto constare non censetur, nisi:

1° Sententia documentis innitatur, quae postea fuerint falsa deprehensa;

2° Postea detecta fuerint documenta, quae facta nova et contrariam decisionem exigentia peremptorie probent;

3° Sententia ex dolo partis prolata fuerit in damnum alterius;

4° Legis praescriptum evidenter neglectum fuerit.

Canon 1905 allows the use of *restitutio in integrum* as an extraordinary remedy against the judicial sentence which cannot be attacked by an appeal or by a plaint of nullity, if it is manifest that the resulting *res iudicata* is evidently unjust and if the general conditions for this remedy are fulfilled.

The requirements of the canon are four: 1) that the sentence has become irrevocably adjudged; 2) that an appeal or plaint of nullity is not available; 3) that the limits of canons 1687-1688 are observed; 4) that the *res iudicata* is manifestly unjust in one of the ways listed in the second paragraph of the canon. These four conditions will be treated in as many articles.

Article I. Res Iudicata

Restitutio in integrum is possible only against a sentence which has become a *res iudicata.* This status is attained when a sentence can no longer be attacked by the ordinary remedy of appeal and is presumed to correspond to the truth and to be just so that it has the force of law between the litigants.[1] That *restitutio* can be used only against a sentence which has already become thus irrevocably adjudged is clear from canon 1905, § 1—*dummodo de evidenti iniustitia rei iudicatae manifesto constet.* The reason is equally clear. A sentence which is not irrevocably adjudged can still be attacked by the ordinary remedy of appeal; the extraordinary one is unnecessary. Or if the sentence is such that it never becomes a *res iudicata,* a rehearing of the case is always allowed by law. The causes which do not admit a *res iudicata* are those concerning the status of persons—i. e., discussions of the bond of matrimony, of the validity of ordination or religious profession; in these cases, no matter how many sentences have been passed, the question can always be reopened if new and grave arguments or documents are produced.[2] *Resti-*

[1] Canons 1880, 4°, 1904; cf. Roberti, *De Processibus,* II, 243; Lemieux, *The Sentence in Ecclesiastical Procedure,* The Catholic University of America Canon Law Studies, n. 87, (Washington: Catholic University, 1934), p. 101.

[2] Canon 1903; cf. canons 1989, 1998, § 2.

tutio in integrum is therefore not granted as a remedy against a definitive sentence in a case concerning the validity of the marriage bond. Though there may have been some doubt before the Code as to the need of this remedy to reopen such a case, there is no doubt in the law of the Code.[3]

Canon 1902 gives the reasons for which a sentence becomes irrevocably adjudged as follows: 1) if it was confirmed by a second sentence; 2) if it was not appealed, as is allowed by canon 1881, in ten days from the notification of its publication; or if, though the sentence was legitimately appealed, the prosecution of the case has been deserted in the appeal court. The latter case would occur if the appeal action were not commenced in a month[4] or were allowed to languish without a processual act being placed for a full year;[5] 3) if it was a sentence from which the law allows to appeal.

Article II. Appeal and Plaint of Nullity

Restitutio in integrum cannot be invoked against the sentence when one of the ordinary remedies, appeal or plaint of nullity, is available—*adversus sententiam contra quam non suppetat ordinorium remedium appellationis aut guerelae nullitatis.* This is an application of the principle that an extraordinary remedy cannot be used when an ordinary one is open. For appeal and plaint of nullity exhaust the possibilities of an ordinary remedy against

[3] Cf. Supr. Trib. Signaturae Ap., *Paderbornen., nullitatis matrimonii,* 13 maii 1919—*AAS,* XI (1919), 295-297; Oesterle, "De Restitutione in Integrum," *Jus Pontificium,* XVIII (1939), 174-185.

Restitutio is possible, however, and sometimes very useful within a marriage trial to revoke judicial acts according to canons 1687-1688, or even a decree or interlocutory sentence of the judge according to the present canon. Cf. Haring, *Apollinaris,* XI (1938), 296-298. The statements of Dolan that this remedy "will be of no use to the Defensor Vinculi" and that "this remedy will never serve the Defensor Vinculi as a means of furthering his case" require some modification—*The Defensor Vinculi,* The Catholic University of America Canon Law Studies, n. 85, (Washington: Catholic University, 1934), p. 99.

[4] Canon 1883.

[5] Canon 1736.

the sentence as far as the two original parties to the suit are concerned. The *oppositio tertii* is also an extraordinary remedy, but is of no avail to the parties of the case.[6] The correction of the sentence referred to in canon 1878 is used only for material errors in it. To determine the possibility of using *restitutio in integrum,* then, it will be necessary to note the limits set by the law for the appeal and the plaint of nullity.

I. An appeal, or the demand that a higher court reconsider the case to see if the sentence is to stand or to be reformed, is possible against any sentence unless the law forbids it.[7] An appeal is not allowed by the law in certain cases. Against all such sentences, the other conditions being fulfilled, *restitutio* is possible. There can be no appeal, according to canon 1880, from the following sentences:

1) The sentence of the Supreme Pontiff or of the Apostolic Signatura. *Restitutio* is theoretically possible, but only from the judge who passed the sentence.[8]

2) The sentence of a judge delegated by the Holy See with the clause *appeallatione remota.* Such a sentence could, however, be revoked by *restitutio.*[9]

3) A sentence which is null. *Restitutio,* however, is possible only if the plaint of nullity, as well as the appeal, is unavailable.

4) A sentence which has become irrevocably adjudged. This is the reason which most frequently excludes the making of an appeal and therefore the most frequent reason for the employment of *restitutio.* The causes for the *res iudicata* have already been noted.

5) A definitive sentence based on a decisory oath.[10] *Restitutio*

[6] Cf. canons 1898-1901.

[7] Canon 1879.

[8] Canon 1906. For concessions of this remedy against the sentence of a Pope, cf. cc. 4, 5, X, *de in integrum restitutione,* I, 41.

[9] Cf. Connolly, *Appeals,* p. 75; Coronata, *Institutiones,* III, n. 1409; Augustine, *A Commentary on Canon Law,* VII, 320. Such a clause is not in frequent use at present—Roberti, *De Processibus,* II, 199.

[10] Cf. canons 1834-1836.

is possible if it can be proved that the party making the oath perjured himself.[11]

6) A decree or interlocutory sentence which has no definitive force. A decree of the judge is any pronouncement which is not a sentence; it may merely concern the ordering of the process or it may define an incidental question.[12] An interlocutory sentence, in contradistinction to a definitive one which decides the principal issue, decides only an incidental question.[13] If the decree or interlocutory sentence has the force of a definitive sentence, that is, if it precludes the issuing of a definitive one or prejudices the definitive one in any way, then *restitutio in integrum* can be invoked against it.[14] What if the sentence or decree has not definitive force? If it actually causes grave damage to a person—which is hardly conceivable because of the unimportance of the matters which can be settled in this way—then *restitutio* should be allowed against it since it does become irrevocably adjudged and no appeal is possible.[15]

7) A sentence in a cause for which the law demands expeditious treatment. The distinctions just made concerning interlocutory sentence applies also to this type of sentence.[16]

8) A sentence pronounced against a contumacious party who has not purged himself of contempt. This is true only if the

[11] Cf. canon 1905, § 2, 3°; Coronata, *Institutiones,* III, n. 1409; Connolly, *Appeals,* p. 79.

[12] Cf. canons 1868, § 2; 1840; Roberti, *De Processibus,* II, 171-172, I; 297.

[13] Canon 1868, § 1.

[14] "Itaque beneficium restitutionis in integrum . . . non modo scilicet contra definitivam, sed contra interlocutoriam quoque, atque etiam contra iudiciale decretum quod vim habeat definitivae, seu influat in definitivam, dummodo non admittat ordinarium remedium appellationis aut querelae nullitatis"—S. R. Rota, *Poenarum . . . et restitutionis in integrum,* 30 iulii 1930, dec. XLIV, n. 10—*Decisiones,* XXII (1930), 501; cf. also *Competentiae,* 27 apr. 1928, dec. XIV, n. 2, II—*Decisiones,* XX (1928), 139.

[15] Canons 1880, 6°; 1902, 3°; no authority from the Rota or from authors can be cited in favor of this view which is based on the nature of the remedy and the conditions for its use.

[16] Cf. S. R. R., *Poenarum,* 30 iulii 1930, XLIV, n. 10—*Decisiones,* XXII (1930), 501.

person remained in contempt of court to the end of the trial; if he came to court during the trial, he is no longer contumacious and can appeal.[17] If he remains contumacious until after the publication of the sentence he is allowed three months from the day on which he received notice of the passing of the sentence to clear himself of his contempt and to seek a *restitutio in integrum* to appeal.[18]

This restoration of the right to appeal, provided in canon 1847, is entirely independent of canons 1905-1907; in spite of the fact that it is a remedy against a sentence which has become irrevocably adjudged, it is ruled solely by the requirements of canons 1687 and 1688.[19] It is a restoration only to appeal and has not the same effects as the extraordinary remedy against the sentence itself. The appeal would have to be lodged within ten days after the *restitutio* was granted; the case would then have to be retried by the higher court. The time limit for seeking this *restitutio* is curtailed to three months; the day of the notification of the sentence's publication is not counted and the time expires at the end of three months computed as in the calendar.[20] The righteous cause necessary for the extraordinary remedy will be found in the reason given to clear the party of contempt, e. g., that he did not receive the citation, that he was hindered from appearing in court or that he was ignorant of the law. Hanssen

[17] Roberti, *De Processibus,* II, 201.

[18] Canon 1847: "Post latam vero sententiam, contumax beneficium restitutionis in integrum ad appellandum ab ipso iudice qui eam tulit, petere potest, non ultra tamen trimestre ab ipsius sententiae intimatione, nisi agatur de causis quae non transeunt in rem iudicatam."

[19] Lega states that canon 1905 is not to be applied to this restoration to appeal because canon 1847 does not consider a sentence which is irrevocably adjudged; that the causes for its concession are not precisely those of canon 1905; yet, he asserts, the remedy cannot be granted unless one of the causes of canon 1905, § 2, is demonstrated—Lega-Bartoccetti, *op. cit.,* II, 875-876. But a sentence against a contumacious party is irrevocably adjudged by virtue of canon 1880, 8°; and if one of the causes of canon 1905, § 2, is verified, there is no reason for not conceding the remedy against the sentence itself.

at the end of three months computed as in the calendar.[20] The

[20] Canon 34, § 3, 1°, 3°; cf. Roberti, *De Processibus,* II, 136.

holds that because of the nature of the remedy *restitutio* can be given even though the party does not clear himself of contempt; this is true as long as some righteous cause can be offered for the remedy.[21] It seems that even after the three months have elapsed the contumacious party can seek *restitutio* against the sentence during the remainder of a four year period the same as anyone else, if he can demonstrate that all of the requirements of canon 1905 are satisfied.

9) A sentence pronounced aainst a person who has expressly renounced in writing the right to appeal. Roberti[22] and Coronata,[23] without offering any reasons, claim that such a renunciation carries with it the renunciation of all remedies. Connolly, more correctly it seems, insists that it does not.[24] Though a person may forego the ordinary right to appeal, he should not be presumed to forego the right to attack a sentence which is manifestly unjust for one of the reasons listed in canon 1905, § 2.

II. The plaint of nullity is a remedy by which a party attacks the sentence as null because of some substantial defect.[25] Canon 1892 lists three cases in which the sentence is irremediably null: 1) when it has been passed by an absolutely incompetent judge or by a collegiate tribunal not constituted by the number of judges required by law; 2) when one of the parties lacked the right of appearing personally in court; 3) when someone has acted in the name of another without a legitimate mandate. These nullities can be attacked for a period of thirty years by means of a suit for the declaration of the nullity of the sentence.[26]

A sentence may also be only remediably null, according to canon 1894, in one of four ways: 1) when there was lacking a legitimate citation; 2) when the sentence itself is devoid of

[21] "De sanctione nullitatis in processu canonico." *Apollinaris,* XI (1938), 400.

[22] *De Processibus,* II, 202.

[23] *Institutiones,* III, n. 1409.

[24] *Appeals,* p. 88.

[25] Cf. Lemieux, *The Sentence,* p. 96; Coronata, *Institutiones,* III, n. 1417.

[26] Canon 1893.

the reasons for the decision;[27] 3) when the sentence lacks the required signatures; 4) when it lacks indication of the complete date and place in which it was pronounced. The plaint of nullity against a sentence for any of these reasons is available for three months from the date of the publication of the sentence.[28] Whether the listings of nullities in canons 1892 and 1894 are to be regarded as exclusive so that a sentence cannot be impugned as null for any other reason is a question which will be discussed at length in the next chapter. If the plaint of nullity is available, *restitutio* cannot be granted.

Article III. The Limits of Canons 1687-1688

The third condition required for the use of *restitutio* against the sentence is found in the phrase *"intra fines can. 1687, 1688."* This reference to the earlier canons makes applicable to the remedy as used against the sentence everything in them which is not contrary to the regulations of canons 1905-1907. The conditions of canons 1687 and 1688 as applied to the use of the remedy against the sentence are as follows:

1) Adults need a specific righteous cause to receive the benefit of *restitutio* in any case, while minors and moral persons do not.[29] In this specific use of the remedy any one of the reasons for the injustice of the *res iudicata*, as listed in canon 1905, § 2, can be a righteous cause for the employment of *restitutio* in favor of an adult.[30] Although minors ordinarily do not need any other cause than their lack of age, still one of the circumstances of canon 1905, § 2, must be verified before they can invoke the remedy against the sentence.[31]

[27] Exception is made for the Apostolic Signatura by reference to canon 1605.

[28] Canon 1895.

[29] Canon 1687, § 1, § 2.

[30] Wernz-Vidal, *Ius Canonicum*, VI, nn. 318, 641; Muniz, *Procedimientos Eclesiásticos*, III, n. 522.

[31] Roberti, *De Processibus*, II, 254.

2) The adult must moreover prove that the damage is not to be imputed to himself.[32]

3) The right to seek the remedy passes to the heirs and successors of minors and of those who enjoy their rights.[33]

4) The remedy must be sought within four years, from the date of majority in the case of minors and from the time the damage occurred and all hindrances ceased in the case of adults and moral persons.[34] This quadriennium is to be computed as usable time exclusively. Roberti considers it in the nature of usable time in its beginning but as continuous time once the initial impediment has ceased to exist.[35] Since the time limit limit is one of the conditions taken from canon 1688, and since Roberti in his commentary on that canon interprets the time limit as involving usable time both in its beginning and in its course,[36] it is difficult to find any basis for a restriction when the remedy is employed against the sentence. It should be interpreted as usable time in its fullest sense.[37]

5) The remedy can be granted *ex officio* to minors and to moral persons, the promoter of justice being previously consulted in the case.[38]

6) Most important of all the conditions of the earlier canons on the remedy is that there must be *grave* damage which is to be repaired by the *restitutio.* In this use of the remedy the grave damage is not that which would result from the execution of

[32] Canon 1687, § 2; cf. S. R. R., *Restitutionis in integrum et diffamationis,* 16 febr. 1925, dec. XI, n. 2— *Decisiones,* XVII (1925), 83.

[33] Canon 1687, § 1.

[34] Canon 1688, § 1.

[35] *De Processibus,* II, 267.

[36] *De Processibus,* I, 392.

[37] Coronata (*Institutiones,* III, n. 1426) says simply "utile est quadriennium," but cites Roberti in a footnote. The interpretation of Wernz-Vidal (*Ius Canonicum,* VI, n. 641) and Muniz (*Procedimientos Eclesiásticos,* III, n. 522) is not clear; they state merely that the time runs for adults from the day the sentence becomes irrevocably adjudged or from the time the hindrance ceases.

[38] Canon 1688, § 2.

the sentence.[39] Every judicial sentence involves some damage, and often a grave damage, for one or the other party. *Restitutio* is specifically invoked not to repair such damage, but rather to repair the injustice of the *res iudicata.* The remedy, if granted, will perhaps eventually repair the damage which the execution of the sentence would inflict upon the condemned party, but its direct effect is to repair the grave damage inherent in an unjust sentence.[40] And in this sense grave damage will result only from grave injustice.

7) One notable exception to the general law on *restitutio* is that minors here have no choice of remedies. The adage, "To one having an ordinary remedy, an extraordinary one is not to be given," admits no modification in favor of minors and moral persons. This is apparent from the wording of canon 1905, § 1. Although this canon does state "within the limits of canons 1687, 1688," this phrase follows after the prerequisite condition for the use of the remedy against the sentence—the exclusion of appeal or plaint of nullity; the latter phrase in the canon cannot be interpreted to limit the general norm laid down immediately prior to it. Coronata, however,[41] and Besson [42] retain this right of choice for minors from the old law. It is true that no author directly contradicts their opinion, though Coronata notes that Roberti [43] implies the opposite. So do all other commentators by omitting this distinction, which, if warranted, would be worthy of notice.

8) Another exception is that canon 1906 lays down particular rules for the competence of the judge who can concede the remedy against the sentence.

[39] Thus Wernz-Vidal, *Ius Canonicum,* VI, n. 641.

[40] ". . . qui notabiliter laesus est, ob evidentem rei iudicatae iniustitiam"—Coronata, *Institutiones,* III, n. 1426; "Sane institutum restitutionis constantem finem habuit reparandi iniustitias"—Roberti, *De Processibus,* II, 261.

[41] *Institutiones,* III, nn. 1426, 1427.

[42] "Sur la Restitution 'in integrum',"—*Nouvelle Revue Theéologique,* XLVII (1920), 468.

[43] *De Processibus,* II, 254.

Article IV. The Injustice of the Res Iudicata

The injustice of the *res iudicata* is the fourth and last condition laid down in canon 1905, § 1, for employing *restitutio* as a remedy against the sentence. The canon states "*dummodo de evidenti iniustitia rei iudicatae manifesto constet.*" The extraordinary remedy is allowed to prevent a party from being permanently oppressed by an unassailable sentence which is unjust.[44]

The canon seems almost repetitious in its demand that the injustice be obvious: *de evidenti iniustitia . . . manifesto constet.* The force of the *res iudicata* is not to be discarded for the sake of a mere suspicion of injustice. As the Rota has noted, the demands of the law in this respect have been made more rigorous by the Code. Whereas previously the injustice of a sentence could be demonstrated by ordinary means of proof, now the injustice must be manifest.[45] The Signatura likewise noted that the grounds for asserting the injustice of the sentence must be demonstrated by "clear and univocal proofs." [46] And the Rota remarks that "simple or natural injustice will not suffice but it must be compelling."[47] Moreover, the phrase requiring the evident injustice to be manifest is introduced by *dummodo* to show that it is a *sine qua non* condition.[48]

The innovation of the Code is even greater. It not only requires the injustice to be manifest, but it takes the matter of

[44] The canon speaks of the injustice of the *res iudicata.* In the face of the *praesumptio iuris et de iure* in favor of the *res iudicata* stated in the preceding canon, 1904, § 1, it would seem that canon 1905 would read more exactly if it said "only when the evident injustice of the sentence is manifest" rather than "only when the evident injustice of the *res iudicata* is manifest." Canon 1905 at first sight admits direct proof against that which has the strongest possible presumption in its favor—the justice of the *res iudicata*—and which should, according to canon 1826, admit only indirect proof.

[45] Cf. *Apollinaris,* III (1930), 365, taken from S. R. Rota, *Decisiones,* XI (1919), 76 ff.

[46] *De Manila,* 6 mart. 1920—*AAS,* XII (1920), 257.

[47] ". . . iniustitiam decretoriam."—*Restitutionis in integrum,* 29 mart. 1927, dec. XII, n. 5—*Decisiones,* XIX (1927), 95.

[48] Cf. analogy in canon 39.

deciding what constitutes manifest injustice out of the hands of the individual judge entirely. In the second paragraph of canon 1905 the cases in which the injustice will be manifest are given in an exhaustive list.[49] No judge can validly grant a *restitutio* against a sentence except when one of these circumstances be verified. The canon employs the adverb *nisi* to demonstrate that the list is an exhaustive one and states its proposition in the negative to emphasize its prohibitive force: *"De iniustitia autem manifesto constare non censetur, nisi. . ."* Four possible grounds are given for accusing the status of *res iudicata* of being manifestly unjust. Three of them concern errors of fact; one concerns an error of law.

A. *False Documents*

Canon 1905.—§ 2. De iniustitia autem manifesto constare non censetur, nisi:

1° Sententia documentis innitatur, quae postea fuerint falsa deprehensa;

The sentence may be unjust if it is based on documents which are afterwards discovered to be false.[50] First, it is essential that the sentence be based on the documents which are false. Even though it can be proved that false documents were presented in the trial *restitutio in integrum* cannot be granted unless the sentence were based on them. The judge may have attained the moral certitude on which he decided the case because of the testimony of witness or because of other documents presented besides those now proved to be false. How can one tell whether the sentence was based on the false documents? If the judge has observed the law, the motives for his deeision will be expressed in the sentence.[51] If the false documents were one of the motives

[49] Cf. S. R. R., *Luganen.*, 16 febr. 1925, dec. XI, n. 2—*Decisiones*, XVII (1925), 83; Roberti, *De Processibus*, II, 253; Vermeersch-Cruesen, *Epitome*, III, n. 246.

[50] Cf. c. 5, X, *de in integrum restitutione*, I, 41; S. C. C. *Lauretana*, 17 dec. 1887—*ASS*, XX (1887), 487.

[51] Canons 1873, § 1, 3°; 1894, 2°; cf. Woywod, "Reinstatement in Former Position," *Hom. Past. Rev.*, XXXIII (1932-1933), 376.

for the decision, it must be determined whether they were the chief motive. If the sentence would have been the same if the false documents had never been presented, *restitutio* should not be given.

The documents in question can be either public or private ones.[52] It will be more difficult to prove public documents to be false because, as canon 1814 states, they are presumed genuine until the contrary is demonstrated with evident arguments.[53] The documents need not be proved spurious or apocryphal, however; by false documents is meant documents which contain something false. Even an apocryphal document can contain truth, though its probative force is greatly weakened by not being genuine. Likewise a genuine document can be shown not to contain the truth without contesting its genuinity.[54] Though *documentis* in the text is plural, one false document if it were decisive in the case—e. g., a last will and testament in a case on succession—would be sufficient to warrant the concession of *restitutio*. It does not matter which party has presented the documents; but if the petitioner himself has presented them, he must have acted in good faith, thinking them to tell the truth.[55]

Since oral testimony given in the trial will have been incorporated into the acts of the case,[56] false testimony will fall under the heading of false documents if its untruthfulness is manifest from the authentic acts of the case.[57] Perjured testimony might moreover be the ground for *restitutio* under canon 1905, § 2, 3°.

Second, the falsity of the documents must be discovered after the sentence has become irrevocably adjudged—*quae postea fuerint*

[52] Cappello, *Summa Iuris Canonici*, III, n. 361; Coronata, *Institutiones*, III, n. 1427; Woywod, *loc. cit.* For definitions of documents, cf. canons 1812-1818.

[53] Cf. Wernz-Vidal, *Ius Canonicum*, VI, n. 639.

[54] Cf. Coronata, *Institutiones*, III, n. 1427; Roberti, *De Processibus*, II, 98.

[55] Cf. Woywod, *Hom. Past. Rev.*, XXXIII (1932-1933), 376.

[56] Canon 1778.

[57] Cf. Roberti, *De Processibus*, II, 255; Coronata, *Institutiones*, III, n. 1427.

falsa deprehensa. Application is here made to both minors and adults of the principle of canon 1687, § 2, that the petitioner for the remedy must not be the cause of the damage he has suffered. If during the course of the trial he became aware that false documents had been presented to the court and yet held his peace, the damage is to be imputed to him. Others may indeed have previously known of their falsity; it is enough that the petitioner learn of this not only after the sentence has been handed down but also after it has become irrevocably adjudged. Such is the force of the word *postea* in the text, for the discovery of the falsity of the proofs is to show the injustice of the *res iudicata.*[58] As a result, if during the ten days allowed for appeal a party learns that the sentence against him was based on false documents, he must use this knowledge as a ground for an appeal; if he fails to appeal, his petition for *restitutio* should not be heard, because he is the cause of the damage he suffers.

B. *New Documents*

Canon 1905.—§ 2. De iniustitia autem manifesto constare non censetur, nisi:

2° Postea detecta fuerint documenta, quae facta nova et contrariam decisionem exigentia peremptorie probent;

The injustice of the *res iudicata* is manifest if later there are found new documents which decisively prove new facts and therefore demand a contrary decision. Documents are considered new when they have not been presented previously in the trial. *Postea* again points to a time after the sentence has become irrevocably adjudged. If the petitioner were aware of their existence and their bearing on the case before this time, they cannot be said to be *postea detecta;* the petitioner is not to be heard.[59] *Documenta* cannot be extended to include new witnesses. No writer has attempted to interpret the canon thus. True, in canon 1990 proof of the existence of an impediment is demanded *"ex certo et*

[58] Vermeersch-Cruesen, *Epitome,* III, n. 246; Roberti, however, says merely *"post sententiam"—De Processibus,* II, 254.

[59] Cf. Cocchi, *De Processibus,* n. 241.

authentico documento," yet authors allow proof by witnesses in lieu of documentary proof when the latter cannot be procured.[60] An argument from analogy, however, should not prompt a judge to admit an irrevocably adjudged case to a rehearing through a *restitutio in integrum* for the sake of new witnesses. The petitioner must certainly have at least known of the existence of other witnesses during the trial and should have asked to have their testimony heard; this he could have done by asking for a delay, if necessary;[61] or if the possible witnesses were in another place at the time, through the services of another court.[62] Since public or private documents are acceptable,[63] a party could, if he felt that he had found witnesses who could testify to new and convincing facts, have the testimony put in writing and presented as a document.

The new documents must not be mere repetitions of what the court has already considered. They must set forth new facts which were not previously known, though they may have existed.[64] These newly found facts must be convincing since the canon requires that they "demand a contrary decision." This must be properly understood, for *restitutio in integrum* in itself does not give a contrary decision, but merely revokes the existing sentence, so that the way is opened for a new examination of the case. The sentence had applied the law to a state of facts which was considered sufficiently established; if the petitioner can by new documents show that a different state of facts in reality existed, he should be given a chance to be heard again.[65] These new facts

[60] Cf. Gasparri, *Tractatus Canonicus de Matrimonio* (2 ed., 2 vols., Civitate Vaticana: Typis Polyglottis Vaticanis, 1932), n. 1283; Cappello, *Tractatus Canonico-Moralis de Sacramentis,* Vol. III, *De Matrimonio* (4 ed., Taurinorum Augustae: Marietti, 1939), n. 891; Vermeersch-Cruesen, *Epitome,* III, n. 276.

[61] Canon 1634, § 2.

[62] Canons 1570, § 2; 1770, § 1, 3° -4°.

[63] Cf. *Regulae servandae in iudiciis apud Suprem. Signaturae Ap. Tribunal,* 6 mart. 1912, art. 9, b—*AAS,* IV (1912), 190.

[64] Muniz,*Procedimientos Eclesiásticos,* III, n. 520; Wernz-Vidal, *Ius Canonicum,* VI, n. 639.

[65] Cf. Woywod, *Hom. Past. Rev.,* XXXIII, part 1 (1932-1933), 376.

must be peremptorily, that is decisively, proved by the documents; the documents are useless for this purpose if there is doubt about their probative value.[66]

C. *The Fraud of the Other Party*

Canon 1905.—§ 2. De iniustitia autem manifesto constare non censetur, nisi:

3° Sententia ex dolo partis prolata fuerit in damnum alterius;

The injustice of the *res iudicata* is manifest if the sentence was pronounced because of the fraud of one party to the detriment of the other. The fraud must have actually been the cause for the issue being decided as it was; it must be *dolus causam dans* and not *dolus incidens.* This is clear from the wording of the text, *ex dolo . . . prolata.* It must moreover be the fraud of the other party to the trial and not of an outsider, unless that person performed the fraud at the instance of the former; fraud perpetrated by a procurator will frequently redound on the principal.

The most frequent way in which one party could fraudulently influence the court to decide in his favor and against the other is by perjury, that is, by telling lies in answer to the interrogation of the judge in spite of his oath to tell the truth.[67] The sentence would certainly be procured through fraud if it were

Vermeersch-Cruesen (*Epitome,* III, n. 246) require that the probative force of the documents with regard to the necessity of reforming the sentence allow no controversy. Since the effect of the remedy in itself is not to reform the sentence, this interpretation seems too strict. Unfortunately, because canon 1906 renders the Rota incompetent to receive petitions for this remedy on any ground but that of canon 1905, § 2, 4°, no guidance for the interpretation of the other numbers of this canon is to be found in the decisions of that tribunal. Note that canon 1907 allows a provisional execution of the sentence, but demands that a guaranty be given by the party in whose favor this is done; such a provision of the law would be needless if *restitutio* could be given only when there was certainty that the sentence would be reversed.

[66] Cf. Cappello, *Summa Iuris Canonici,* III, n. 361.

[67] Cf. Wernz-Vidal, *Ius Canonicum,* VI, n. 639.

based on a decisory oath in which the party had perjured himself.[68] The same would result from the subornation of witnesses if the sentence were based on their testimony. The petitioner could still seek the remedy if his own procurator were aware of the fraud or even consented to it; his mandate cannot be presumed to extend to the commission of fraud.[69]

D. *The Neglect of a Prescript of Law*

The interpretation of the final clause of canon 1905, § 2, on the neglect of the law; *"4° Legis praescriptum evidenter neglectum fuerit,"* is more acridly disputed than any other question concerning *restitutio in integrum* since the appearance of the Code. The next chapter, therefore, is devoted solely to its consideration.

[68] Cf. canons 1834-1836; Vermeersch-Cruesen, *Epitome,* III, n. 247; Hanssen, *Apollinaris,* XII (1939), 223.

[69] Cf. Badii, "Il Dolo nel Codice,"—*Diritto Ecclesiastico,* XL (1929), 305-326, especially 325-326.

Chapter X

THE NEGLECT OF A PRESCRIPT OF LAW

Canon 1905.—§ 2. De iniustitia autem manifesto constare non censetur, nisi:

4° Legis praescriptum evidenter neglectum fuerit.

The first three clauses of canon 1905, § 2, allow *restitutio* because of the discovery after the sentence has become irrevocably adjudged that the factual basis of the sentence was wholly untenable; some error of fact had intervened. In the last clause *restitutio* is allowed because of some error of law. It is granted because the sentence is considered to be manifestly unjust if the judge had evidently neglected a prescription of the law in the course of the trial. As to the meaning of the words *evidenter neglectum* there is no difficulty. The neglect of a law can be either positive, an action contrary to the law, or negative, an omission of consideration of some law.[1] As the Rota has pointed out, the prohibition of lesser violations contains a prohibition of greater ones, so that by mention of the neglect of a law, the positive violation of one is included.[2]

The neglect of the law must be evident. There must be no question as to the fact that a law was violated or passed over.[3] Nor will the violation of an uncertain law suffice; the law must be clearly recognized in its interpretation. If there is any dispute among the authors as to the requirements of the law, *restitutio* will not be granted for its violation.[4] It is also universally accepted that the words *legis praescriptum* are not to be limited to pre-

[1] Cf. S. R. R., *S. Iacobi de Chile, Restitutionis in integrum et compromissi*, 5 iunii 1927, dec. XXXIV, n. 7—*Decisiones*, XIX (1927), 280; Pellegrini, *Praxis Vicariorum*, pp. 87-88; Roberti, *De Processibus*, II, 257.

[2] S. R. R., *ibid.*, n. 8, p. 281.

[3] S. R. R., *Poenarum . . . et restitutionis in integrum*, 30 iulii 1930, dec. XLIV, n. 11—*Decisiones*, XXII (1930), 501; Coronata, *Institutiones*, III, n. 1427.

[4] Cf. S. R. R., *ibid.*, n. 17, pp. 503-504; *S. Iacobi de Chile*, 5 iunii 1927, dec. XXXIV, n. 12—*Decisiones*, XIX (1927), 283.

scriptions of the common law. The violation of a particular law by which the parties may be bound, e. g., of a statute regulating a pious foundation, or of some condition of a will or contract, is sufficient ground to render the sentence unjust.[5]

But as to what part of the common law is included in the phrase *legis praescriptum* there is no agreement. Roberti [6] and those who follow him [7] exclude from canon 1905, § 2, 4°, the violation of merely formal procedural law. The common opinion, on the other hand, which is usually referred to as that of the late Msgr. Sosio D'Angelo, allows *restitutio in integrum* against a sentence if a violation of a law of procedure has caused grave damage.[8]

[5] Cf. Suprem. Signaturae Ap. Trib., *De Manila, nullitatis et restitutionis in integrum seu legati pii,* 6 apr. 1920—*AAS,* XII (1920), 257.

[6] *De Processibus,* II, 258-263; "Circa limites querelae nullitatis et restitutionis in integrum,"—*Apollinaris,* I (1928), 476-483; *Consultationes Iuris Canonici,* I (Romae: Pont. Inst. Utriusque Iuris, 1934), n. LXXV, pp. 244-245.

[7] Lemieux, *The Sentence in Ecclesiastical Procedure,* pp. 99, 102; Julien, "Compromissum in arbitros iuxta Codicem Iuris Canonici,"—*Apollinaris,* X (1937), 566; Hanssen, "De sanctione nullitatis in processu canonico,"—*Apollinaris,* XII (1939), 238-249.

[8] D'Angelo, "Un caso di 'restitutio in integrum'," reprinted in *Saggi su Questioni giuridiche* (Torino: Lega Italiana Cattolica Editrice, 1928), pp. 119-126, from *Ephemerides Theologicae Lovanienses,* III (1926), 355-360; "De Restitutione in Integrum,"—*Periodica,* XVIII (1929), 37*-62*; Blat, *De Processibus,* n. 438; Wernz-Vidal, *Ius Canonicum,* VI, nn. 623, 639; Glynn, *The Promoter of Justice,* p. 317; Coronata, *Institutiones,* III, n. 1427; Vermeersch-Creusen, *Epitome,* III, n. 246; Woywod, *Hom. Past. Rev.,* XXXIII (1932-1933), 377; Cappello, *Summa Iuris Canonici,* III, n. 361; Muniz, *Procedimientos Eclesiásticos,* III, nn. 505, 520; Cavigioli, *Manuale di Diritto Canonico* (Torino: Societa Editrice Internazionale, 1934), p. 654, note 1; Romani, *Il Monitore Ecclesiastico,* 5. series, VIII (1936), 82. By the examples which they give the following must be adjudged as holding the same opinion—Eichmann, *Das Prozessrecht des Codex Iuris Canonici,* p. 187; Sipos, *Euchiridion Iuris Canonici,* n. 210; Pruemmer, *Manuale Iuris Canonici* (4-5 ed., Friburgi Brisgoviae: Herder, 1927), p. 613. Likewise Haring *(Grundzüge des katholischen Kirchenrectes* [3 ed., 2 vols., Graz: Ulrich Mosers, 1924], II, 886) allows *restitutio* for "Nichtbeachtung der Prozesszvorschrift;" and Koeniger *(Katholisches Kirchenrecht* [Frieburg im Briesgau: Herder, 1926], p. 421) says "im Falle eines Formfehlers des Urteils. . ."

The question is intimately connected with that of the interpretation of canons 1892 and 1894 on the limits of the *querela nullitatis*. Roberti [9] holds that the list of causes entailing the nullity of a sentence given in these canons is not all-inclusive; that a sentence may be null for other reasons and can consequently be attacked by a plaint of nullity. Most of the writers who hold with D'Angelo that *restitutio* can be used against a sentence because of the neglect of a prescription of procedural law maintain that the use of the *querela* is strictly limited to cases of canons 1892 and 1894.

The interpretations given to the canons on the two remedies are not, however, necessarily dependent.[10] One writer, Crnica, holds that neither the canons on the plaint of nullity nor the words *legis praescriptum* admit an extensive interpretation; that the Code is therefore defective because it offers no remedy for a sentence vitiated by a violation of procedural law which is not listed in canons 1892, 1894.[11] This opinion, however forcefully presented, simply begs the question and is no aid in interpreting the law at present.

The two opposing views will be stated with the chief arguments of their proponents. After an appraisal of these views, a practical conclusion will be attempted. For the sake of brevity the opinions will be referred to as the restrictive interpretation, represented by Roberti, and the extensive interpretation, defended by D'Angelo. Due credit, wherever necessary, will be given to the contributions of others to each opinion.

[9] *De Processibus*, II, 228-231.

[10] Of the authors cited in note 8, *supra*, as holding *restitutio* possible for violations of procedural law, the following expressly state that the canons on the plaint of nullity are exclusive—D'Angelo, *Periodica*, XVIII (1929), 41*-44*; Wernz-Vidal, *Ius Canonicum*, VI, n. 623; Muniz, *Procedimientos Eclesiásticos*, III, n. 505; Coronata, *Institutiones*, III, n. 1418. On the other hand Lega states that the listing of nullities in canon 1894 is not all-inclusive; but he does not exclude formal procedural laws from the term *legis praescriptum* since he considers *restitutio* possible against a sentence which was remediably null but which has been sanated by the lapse of three months—Lega Bartoccetti, *op. cit.*, II, 1022, 1025-1026.

[11] "Defectus Codicis I. C. in designandis normis pro querela nullitatis," *Jus Pontificium*, XV (1935), 145-155.

Article I. Restrictive Interpretation

Only the violation of those rules governing procedure which are substantive law will warrant the use of *restitutio in integrum* against the definitively adjudicated sentence because of its injustice. Procedural laws include all those which regulate the judicial process; most of them, however, are merely formal; they are to be regarded as the form related to the substantive law. Such are all those laws regulating the constitution of tribunals, the capacity of the parties, the form of judicial acts, the *fatalia,* etc. But there are some procedural laws which are substantive because they govern the distribution of goods, e. g., the laws conceding actions.[12] For the violation of a substantive law of procedure *restitutio* is to be granted in virtue of canon, 1905, § 2, 4°; for the violation of a merely formal procedural law, *restitutio* is not to be given, but a *querela nullitatis* is possible. This follows from the fact that the enumeration of canons 1892 and 1894 is non exclusive and also from the very wording of canon 1905, § 2.

First, the canons which list the causes for the plaint of nullity do not exclude the possibility of other causes. Canon 1679 allows an action for the declaration of the nullity of any act. Canon 1680, § 2, makes a distinction between the nullity of an act which is intrinsic to it and the nullity which is derived from the invalidity of an earlier act on which it depends. In the law on processes there are many formalities required under sanction of nullity of the acts of the trial. For example, those acts which are not signed by a notary are declared null in canon 1585, § 1; or, according to canon 1587, § 1, the acts performed in a case wherein the presence of the promoter of justice or of the defender of the bond is necessary are null if that official was not cited or at least present. Since the sentence depends on the acts of the case,[13] it is null because of a derived nullity if it is the conclusion of an invalid process. The sentence is hardly to be

[12] Roberti, *De Processibus,* II, 253; I, 35; *Apollinaris,* I (1928), 479; Hanssen, *Apollinaris,* XII, (1939), 242.

[13] The judge must acquire the moral certitude on which he bases the sentence *"ex actis et probatis"*—Canon 1869, § 2.

exempted for the general rules of canons 1679-1680. Other laws which if violated would nullify the process and therefore the sentence are found in canons 1861, § 2, 1740, § 2, etc.[14] Violations of the natural law as well as of the positive law will nullify a sentence. This has been asserted by the Signatura and the Rota several times since the promulgation of the Code.[15]

Any sentence which is null because it terminates an invalid process is to be attacked by a plaint of nullity in spite of the fact that it is not provided for in canons 1892, 1894. Most of the nullities, especially those of the positive law, will be remediable; if the party aggrieved does not take exception to such nullity, he is presumed to renounce his right and the nullity is sanated after the lapse of the three month period allowed by canon 1895.[16] This is not the only case in the Code of a demonstrative list which appears to be all-inclusive. The enumeration in canon 1902 of the cases which constitute a *res iudicata* is not all-inclusive for it omits any provision for cases of appeal in which there has intervened either an abatement or a renunciation; yet in these cases the sentence of the first court becomes irrevocably adjudged.[17]

Furthermore, canon 1905, § 2, 4° does not contemplate violations of formal procedural law:

1) *Legis praescriptum* respects only substantive law in spite of the fact that as a general term it seems to refer to any law; the meaning of the term is to be derived from the whole canon. The reason for *restitutio* against the sentence is the manifest injustice of the sentence. A violation of formal procedural law would render a sentence not unjust but illegitimate. Thus the

[14] Roberti, *De Processibus*, II, 229-230; *Apollinaris*, I (1928), 477-479; Hanssen, *Apollinaris*, XII (1939), 240-242.

[15] Signatura: *De Manila*, 6 apr. 1920—*AAS*, XII (1920), 256; *Paderbornen.*, 10 martii 1919,—*AAS*, XI (1919), 296-297. S. R. R.: *Mauranen. seu Camberien.*, 13 iulii 1918—*AAS*, XI (1919), 395. Cf. Hanssen, *ibid.*, p. 246.

[16] Roberti, *De Processibus*, II, 230; Hanssen, *ibid.*, pp. 247-248.

[17] Canons 1736, 1741; cf. Roberti, *De Processibus*, II, 228; *Apollinaris*, I (1928), 477.

Code refers to acts placed in violation of formal laws as illegitimate in canons 1723, 1892, nn. 1 and 3, and 1894, n. 1; the Code likewise distinguishes between unjust and illegitimate sentences in canon 1654, § 1, and between null and unjust acts in canons 1624, § 1, 1603, § 1, 1°. It must be concluded that the violation of formal laws renders an act illegitimate or null; the violation of substantive law renders the act unjust. This is borne out by the context of canon 1905. The first three reasons for admitting the injustice of the sentence regard the merits of the cause. So too should the fourth. A sentence will be unjust because of a neglect of law only when the law is one regarding the merits of the case.[18]

2) The purpose of *restitutio* is to repair injustice. But no injustice is repaired by granting the remedy for a violation of procedural law. The new sentence will confirm the old. Moreover, abuses will be frequent, for the other interpretation allows too great freedom to the individual judge in discerning which violations beget grave damage.[19]

3) Historically this opinion is the better founded. The cause for *restitutio* under discussion was introduced into the courts of the Papal States from the French court of cassation during the French invasion of Italy; when the tribunal of cassation was abolished in 1816, the Signatura took over some of its prerogatives, including that of granting *restitutio in integrum* as a result of the violation of law.[20] But this power of the Signatura was limited to the use of *restitutio* for violations of substantive law, as Hanssen has demonstrated from a letter of the Papal Secretary of State found in the Vatican Archives.[21] Later the *Regolamento*

[18] Roberti, *De Processibus,* II, 260; Hanssen, *Apollinaris,* XII (1939), 242; Crnica, *Jus Pontificium,* XV (1935), 152.

[19] Roberti, *De Processibus,* II, 261; *Apollinaris,* I (1928), 481.

[20] ". . . per una ingiustizia, che resulti o dal non essersi avuta ragione nei giudicati di qualche legge, o dall' essersi manifestamente contravvenuta ad una legge vigente."—Pius VII, Motu Proprio, *"Reformatio publicae administrationis et tribunalium ditionis Pontificiae,"* 6 iulii 1816, art. 53—*Bull. Rom. Cont.,* XIV, 53. This argument is evolved by Hanssen, *Apollinaris,* XII (1939), 242-244.

[21] ". . . di qualche legge riguardante il merito del giudizio"—letter to

of Gregory XVI, promulgated in 1834 for the Papal States, allowed *restitutio* for the violation of law; but it made a distinction between *restitutio* for the neglect of substantive law [22] and *restitutio* for the neglect of formal procedural law, which latter it limited to cases in which the sentence lacked motivation, or the reasons for the decision were not stated, or the legal time limits had not been observed in the trial.[23]

It cannot be argued, then, that because the fourth fragment of canon 1905, § 2, resembles the law of Gregory XVI, it is therefore meant to include procedural law; canon 1905, § 2, 4°, does resemble the Gregorian law, but it resembles it in that section which refers to the substantive law or the merits of the case. The *Regulae* of the Signatura of 1912 made the violation of law—whether it be substantive or merely formal—a ground for the plaint of nullity.[24] If from the viewpoint of the opponents' opinion it be granted that canon 1905 follows the Gregorian code rather than the rules of the Signatura,[25] then it must still be admitted that it follows the law of Gregory which referred to a violation of substantive law.

Article II. Extensive Interpretation

According to this view, *legis praescriptum* in canon 1905 is meant to include violations of formal procedural law.

the Legate at Bologna, dated Jan. 21, 1817, cited by Hanssen, *loc. cit.*, note 55.

22 "La ingiustizia manifesta dee resulta . . . o dal non essersi nelle sentenze avuto ragione di qualche legge; o dall' essersi espressamente contravvenuta ad una legge in vigore."—§ 1058—*Acta Gregorii Papae XVI*, IV, 365.

23 "La inosservanza delle forme prescritte dalle leggi di procedura potra ritenersi dal tribunale supremo come violazione di legge, all' effetto di accordare la restitutio in integrum ne' seguenti casi: 1) Se i tribunali non hanno dato per iscritto le ragioni di dubitare e di decidere; 2) Se le sentenze non sono motivate; 3) Se non furono osservati i termini sustanziali del giudizio."—§ 1059, *loc. cit.*

24 *Regulae servandae in iudiciis apud Suprem. Signaturae Ap. Tribunal*, 6 mart. 1912, art 4, d, e.—*AAS*, IV (1912), 189.

25 D'Angelo, *Saggi*, p. 124; Cocchi, *Commentarium in Codicem Iuris Canonici, Liber IV, De Processibus* (Taurinorum Augustae: Marietti, 1930), n. 241.

1) This can be demonstrated by a proper interpretation of the canon, attained through the means of interpretation recommended by canon 18.[26]

a) The text. The words "prescript of law" are general; the law makes no modification, and where the law does not distinguish, neither should we distinguish.

b) The context. *Restitutio* is given only when appeal and plaint of nullity are impossible; the implication is that the extraordinary remedy can be used in circumstances in which the plaint of nullity could have been used for a certain period of time; but the plaint of nullity is intended for violations of formal law.

c) The purpose of the law. *Restitutio* is an extraordinary remedy to be used in a few cases which must be certain. These cases cannot be certain if authors attempt to make subtle distinctions in law: merely formal and substantive procedural laws, etc. Furthermore, if the discussion on the concession of this remedy must concern the merits of the case, in what does it differ from an appeal? The purpose was moreover to rearrange the remedies against the sentence, cutting down the number of nullities.[27]

d) The mind of the legislator. Procedural laws are imposed to be observed. Only the Holy Office is exempted by canon 1555. Since many and serious demands of the procedural law are not listed in canons 1892, 1894, there would be no remedy in case they were neglected unless it were by *restitutio in integrum.* Such, for example, are: the intervention of the notary required in canon 1585; the presence of the promoter of justice or of the defender of the bond as demanded by canon 1587; the constitution of the appeal tribunal according to canons 1595-1596; the alteration of the *libellus,* forbidden in canon 1731, etc. To say that the Code provides no remedy to protect a party against the neglect of these laws is to do injury to the law.

2) The same conclusion is reached through an examination

[26] D'Angelo, "De Restitutione in Integrum," *Periodica,* XVIII (1929), 50*-55*.

[27] D'Angelo, *Saggi,* p. 123.

of the sources of the law.[28] Those sources, cited in the footnotes of the Code to canon 1905, § 2, 4°, concern for the greater part violations of procedural law. For example, from the *Decretals* the cases include one in which the issue was not joined; [29] another in which the sentence was pronounced *"contra leges canonesque;"* [30] still another in which the form of a process was violated.[31] A part of the Constitution *"Ad militantis"* of Benedict XIV is also cited as a source. In this Constitution the Pope decreed as automatically null and void any citations or other procedural acts if the appellate judge violated the procedural forms in accepting a case.[32] And a case before the Sacred Congregation of the Council is cited in which the nullity of the sentence rose from the hearing of unsworn witnesses and the slighting of the testimony of the accused.[33]

Finally, the *Regulae* of the Signatura are noted in which under the motives of nullity are given the lack of consideration of some law and the manifest violation of any law.[34] Whereas in the *Regolamento* of Gregory XVI the violation or neglect of law was the basis for *restitutio in integrum,*[35] in the *Regulae* of the Signatura it was the basis for the plaint of nullity; the Code makes such violations once more the basis for *restitutio.*

[28] D'Angelo, *Periodica,* XVIII (1929), 44*-48*.

[29] C. 2, X, *ut lite non contestata non procedatur ad testium receptionem vel ad sententiam definitivam,* II, 6.

[30] C. 1, X, *de sententia et re iudicata,* II, 27.

[31] ". . . praetermisso iuris ordine"—c. 15, X, *de purgatione canonica,* V, 34; D'Angelo *(loc. cit.)* also cites c. 9, X, *de sententia et re iudicata,* II, 27; c. 5, X, *de feriis,* II, 9.

[32] Benedict XIV, const. *"Ad militantis,"* 30 mart. 1742, § 43—*Fontes,* n. 326.

[33] S. C. C., *Premislien.,* 18 iun., 20 aug. 1887, ad 1—*Fontes,* n. 4271.

[34] *Regulae servandae in iudiciis apud Suprem. Signaturae Ap. Tribunal,* 6 mart. 1912, art. 4, d, e—*AAS,* IV (1912), 189. This argument from the footnotes of the Gasparri edition of the Code was first proposed in an abbreviated form by Blat—*De Processibus,* n. 438. The Rota incorporated it verbatim without citation from D'Angelo (*Periodica,* XVIII [1929], 46*-47*) in a decision wherein it embraced this opinion—*S. Iacobi de Chile, Restitutionis in integrum et compromissi,* 5 iun. 1927, dec. XXXIV, n. 7—*Decisiones,* XIX (1927), 280-281.

[35] § 1058, for the text of. footnote 22, *supra.*

The clause on the violation of law is to be interpreted, therefore, as it was in the rules of the Signatura, to mean the violation of any law, including merely formal procedural law.[36]

3) Reason demands the same conclusion. A rigid interpretation of canon 1905, § 2, 4°, would leave the victims of a judicial violation of procedural law without remedy.

4) The jurisprudence of the Roman tribunals can be cited in favor of this opinion.[37]

On the other hand, a plaint of nullity cannot be invoked to attack a sentence for any violation of procedural law which is not listed in canons 1892 and 1894; the listing of nullities in those canons is all-inclusive. This is apparent from a comparison of the Code with the preparatory *Schema* drawn up in 1914. In that *Schema* the plaint of nullity was to be granted if the *process* was vitiated by any defect of nullity, and an obviously demonstrative list was given because it read "Ipse processus vitio nullitatis est infectus, e. g. . ."[38] In the Code mention of the nullity of the sentence resulting from the nullity of the process was omitted and the list of causes was made all-inclusive. Again, in the same *Schema* the plaint of nullity was to be allowed if the sentence was based on an evident error of fact, and the example given was the discovery that it was based on false documents. This case was certainly transferred, for it now appears in canon 1905, § 2, 1°, as a basis for *restitutio;* so also a transfer was made regarding the neglect of laws which are not mentioned in canons 1892, 1894.[39]

Moreover, Roberti's argument from canon 1680, which speaks in general of the nullity of acts is not admissible; *actus* in that

[36] D'Angelo, *Periodica,* XVIII (1929), 47*, note 23; *Saggi,* p. 124.

[37] The decisions of the Signatura and Rota cited by both sides will be discussed in the next article.

[38] Though D'Angelo (*Periodica,* XVIII [1929], 43*) cites this as can. 390, n. 5, it corresponds rather with can. 403, n. 5 of *Schema F,* as published—*Codicis Iuris Canonici Schemata, Lib. IV De Processibus, I, De Iudiciis in Genere,* p. 437.

[39] D'Angelo, *ibid.,* p. 42*; *Schema F,* can. 403, n. 2—*Codicis Iuris Canonici Schemata, ibid.,* p. 435.

canon refers to an act in the sense of *negotium;* it cannot be extended to mean the judicial sentence.[40]

Article III. Appraisal of the Opinions

The chief arguments of Roberti and Hanssen are that the canons on the plaint of nullity do not give all-inclusive lists of the causes of nullity and that violations of merely procedural laws do not beget injustice which alone allows the use of *restitutio in integrum.*

The contention that the listings of nullities in canons 1892 and 1894 are not all-inclusive has not been sufficiently demonstrated. Canons 1679-1680 do grant an action against any null act, whether because of intrinsic or derived nullity.[41] But this general law is limited by the particular canons on the plaint of nullity. The catalog of defects which allow the *querela* seems all-inclusive; canon 1893, which allows the *querela* against an irremediably null sentence states *"nullitas de qua in can. 1892 proponi protest;"* no other kind of nullity than that mentioned in the previous canon can be attacked according to canon 1893. Likewise canon 1895 even more clearly allows the plaint of nullity *"in casibus de quibus in can. 1894,"* so as to exclude any cases not mentioned in that canon. Further, as Crnica points out, a comparison of these canons with patently demonstrative lists in the Code shows that the grounds for the plaint of nullity are exhaustively stated: Canon 1813, § 1, in giving examples of public documents, states "The principal public ecclesiastical documents are these . . ." and canon 2147, § 2, in noting five reasons for the removal of an irremovable pastor, says "These causes are chiefly the ones which follow. . ." In other canons the use of the sign, *etc.,* clearly marks a demonstrative list, e. g., in canons 1629, § 1. 1642,

[40] D'Angelo, *ibid.,* p. 44*.

[41] D'Angelo's attempt (*Periodica,* XVIII [1929], 44*) to limit *actus* in these canons to *negotium* is contrary to the common interpretation which includes under these canons both judicial and extra-judicial acts. Cf. Wernz-Vidal, *Ius Canonicum,* VI, n. 295; Vermeersch-Creusen, *Epitome,* III, n. 105; Coronata, *Institutiones,* III, n. 1210; Ferreres, *Institutiones,* II, n. 612; Noval, *De Iudiciis,* n. 331.

§ 1. Moreover, if the legislator wished to give a purely demonstrative list of the causes of nullity in canons 1892 and 1894, he could have included some general clause like: "The manifest violation of any law." [42]

Furthermore, the analogy which Roberti finds between canon 1902 and the canons on the plaint of nullity is not convincing. In canon 1902 the causes of the *res iudicata* are listed fully and completely. The causes which Roberti claims lie outside this list—the abatement and renuntiation of an appeal case—readily fall into the category of a deserted appeal. And this cause is specifically listed in canon 1902, 2°. [43]

If, therefore, Roberti, wishes to use canon 1680 as the basis for an action of nullity against a sentence in view of a procedural defect, this action must be something altogether distinct from the plaint of nullity of canons 1892 ff. There would, then, be no legal foundation for applying, as he does, the distinction between remediable and irremediable nullity, as found in those canons, to an action granted elsewhere in the Code.

Again, it is not admissible that the violation of a formal procedural law cannot render the sentence unjust. Before the appearance of the Code many sentences were attacked before the Rota and the Sacred Congregation of the Council by *restitutio* because they were null. Nullity, it was argued, is the greatest form of injustice. But most of the nullities of the old law were due to violations of formal procedural law. Even though the Code may have drawn a new distinction between the grounds for the plaint of nullity and those for *restitutio,* it did not change the concept of injustice; the violation of a formal procedural law can still render a sentence unjust. The violation of procedural law is a violation of the party's right to have his case tried according to the law, not only the substantive but also the formal law. Procedural formalities were not imposed by the Church for the sake of pomp but to ensure justice; if they are neglected,

[42] "Defectus Codicis I. C. in designandis normis pro querela nullitatis,"—*Jus Pontificium,* XV (1935), 148-149.

[43] Cf. canons 1736, 1740.

the judge acts more or less unjustly; the injustice is measured by the gravity of the law neglected; a grave violation engenders grave injustice.

Roberti says: "A sentence may be had which labors under many defects of form but is still just."[44] Certainly. So too may the sentence be just even though it is based on false documents or obtained through the fraud of the other party. But, the violation of a grave law of procedure gives rise to a founded suspicion that the judge did not judge justly. Again, Roberti asserts that if a sentence is marred only by a defect of form in the process, the reason for granting *restitutio* is lacking since a new sentence legitimately pronounced will confirm the former sentence.[45] Such an assertion is too sweeping; if a judge violated canon 1655, § 2, by not giving an advocate to a minor, or if he violated canon 1731, n. 1, by changing the *libellus* without consulting the other party, certainly a new hearing of the case could bring a different judgment after the minor has been armed with legal advice or after the case is tried according to the original petition.[46] Moreover, Roberti feels that the extensive interpretation of canon 1905, § 2, 4°, would give an arbitrary rein to the individual judge in determining which violations of the law caused grave damage to the petitioner.[47] His own opinion invites the self-same difficulty. For the question as to which violations of procedural law not listed in canons 1892 and 1894 will render a sentence only remediably null rather than irremediably null will not be beyond dispute.[48]

Finally, Roberti's and Hanssen's appeal to the jurisprudence of

[44] *De Processibus,* II, 260.

[45] *De Processibus,* II, 261.

[46] The requirements of canons 1655, § 2, and 1731, n. 1, do not come under Roberti's definition of substantive laws—*quae bona distribuunt*—nor can any violation of these requirements, even in his opinion, be remedied by the plaint nullity, because they have no nullifying clause which could make any contravention of them result in nullity. Cf. canon 11.

[47] *De Processibus,* II, 261; Hanssen, *Apollinaris,* XII (1939), 247.

[48] "Verum sicuti legislator non potuit recensere omnes causas nullitatis, ita nequivit vel saltem noluit singularum nullitatum sanationem determinare; reliquit scientiae et iurisprudentiae."—Hanssen, *Apollinaris,* XII (1939), 236.

the higher tribunals in behalf of their opinion is inconclusive. The decisions offered [49] are practically all pre-Code decisions. Such decisions can have no bearing on the interpretation of canon 1905, § 2, 4°, which states a new ground for ***restitutio in integrum*** in the common law. The Rota has on different occasions noted that the law has changed.[50] In fact these authors themselves admit a change in the law.[51] Of the decisions handed down since the appearance of the Code several seem to accept the extensive interpretation of the canons on the plaint of nullity. But in the cases decided by the Signatura it is to be noted that the Supreme Tribunal still acts, as it has expressly asserted, according to its own Regulae as interpreted by the Chirograph of Benedict XV.[52] The rules of the Signatura as interpreted by Benedict XV allowed not only an action of nullity against the sentence but also the *circumscriptio* of the sentence, the questions proposed to the Signatura in pre-Code times: *"Sitne nulla rotalis sententia? Sitne locus eius circumscriptioni?"* did not imply a repetitious mode of asking for the same thing; they involved alternate petitions, asking for either a declaration of nullity or the rescission—*circumscriptio*— of the sentence.[53] The Signatura still acts on this interpretation of its own powers [54]

[49] Roberti, *De Processibus,* II, 229-230; *Apollinaris,* I (1928), 477-478; Hanssen, *Apollinaris,* XII (1939), 246.

[50] *S. Iacobi de Chile,* 5 iulii 1927, dec. XXXIV—*Decisiones,* XIX (1927), 278; cf. also *Decisiones,* XI, (1919), 76 ff.

[51] Roberti, *De Processibus,* II, 253, 254; Hanssen, *loc. cit.*

[52] ". . . competentia huius S. T. circa nullitatem sententiarum S. R. Rotae, non coarctatur limitibus can 1892 et 1894 signatis; recursus enim quoque admittitur si lata sententia sit manifesto vel contra legem vel non satis perpensa factorum veritate. Et haec latior competentia patet ex Regulis huius S. T. (art. 4) et ex earum Appendice. . ."—*Romana, sententiae incidentalis,* 7 aug. 1922—*AAS,* XV (1923), 183.

[53] Benedict XV, chirographum *"Attentis expositis,"* 28 iun. 1915 *(Appendix ad regulas servandas in iudiciis apud Suprem. Signaturae Ap. Tribunal,* art. 1)—*AAS,* VII (1915), 320-325; *Fontes,* after n. 6462. Cf. *Le Canoniste Contemporain,* XXXVIII (1915), 420-421; Roberti, *De Processibus,* II, 252, note 1.

[54] ". . . sententia rotalis, cum nec factum pervertit, nec legem violaverit, neque nullitate laborat, neque gladio circumscriptionis iugulanda est"—

and is therefore of no avail as a guide for the interpretation of the law binding on lower tribunals.

Of the Rota decisions cited in favor of Roberti's opinion, one which recognized the nullity of a sentence for other reasons than those listed in canons 1892 and 1894 was rendered soon after the Code went into effect and was decided on the old law; it nowhere cites the Code and speaks of the three nullities of the old law—lack of competence, of citation, and of mandate.[55] A brief decree of the Rota is quoted in which a sentence is declared null and remanded to the inferior court. Although it mentions the absence of the promoter of justice, this decree is based on the plaintiff's lack of processual capacity in a criminal trial, as is evident from the citation of canon 1892, 2°, and not on the absence of the promoter of justice in violation of canon 1587, § 2.[56] One recent decision remarks that a sentence would be null in the case of an illegitimate denial of the right to defend oneself even though that particular cause is not listed in canon 1892, *quia non indiget recenseri*.[57] The case in point was the denial of defense involved in the illegitimate declaration of the contumacy of one of the parties. But a different *turnus* on another case granted *restitutio in integrum* in virtue of canon 1905, § 2, 4°, for this same reason.[58]

What of D'Angelo's arguments? His chief argument against the extensive use of the plaint of nullity is based on one of the *Schemata* of the Code. It is to be noted in favor of this argument that five of the progressive *Schemata* recognized as one of the grounds of the nullity of the sentence the fact that

Paderbornen., 16 maii 1919—*AAS*, XI (1919), 299; "Omni ergo fundamento carebat circumscriptionis postulatio"—*De Manila*, 6 apr. 1920—*AAS*, XII (1920), 257; cf. also the case cited in note 52, *supra*.

[55] *Mauranen. seu Camberien., nullitatis sententiae*, 13 iulii 1918—*AAS*, XI (1919), 392-404.

[56] *Decretum*, 28 iulii 1931—*AAS*, XXIV (1932), 99; quoted by Roberti with argument—*Consultationes Iuris Canonici*, I, 244.

[57] *Proprietatis*, 27 febr. 1930, dec. XI, n. 4—*Decisiones*, XXII (1930), 120.

[58] *Incidentis super contumacia*, 24 iulii 1923, dec. XXI,—*Decisiones*, XV (1923), 180-189.

it was the conclusion of an invalid process occasioned by the violation of procedural law during the hearing of the case. Though this provision was present in *Schema G,* the last one drawn up prior to the Code, it was not included in canon 1892 or canon 1894.[59] It is to be further noted that one of the desires expressed to the preparatory commission by the episcopate was that the number of nullities be cut down.[60]

Of D'Angelo's arguments in favor of his interpretation of *legis praescriptum* one is drawn from the sources of the law as set forth in the footnotes of the Code. Great stress may not be placed on citation in the footnotes.[61] Yet the sources noted under canon 1905, § 2, are not excerpted from the old law on *restitutio in integrum* but from the law on the nullity of the sentence; they demonstrate, therefore, at least the interpretation placed on this canon by those responsible for the addition of the notes; if D'Angelo's interpretation is rejected, the majority of the citations to canon 1905 § 2, are meaningless.

As to the argument from the practice of the Roman tribunals, the interpretation of D'Angelo has been completely accepted by the Sacred Roman Rota in one decision handed down in 1927 in a case from Santiago, Chile.[62] The rector of the Santiago seminary had agreed to sell to a layman, Arthur Zavala, a plot of ground belonging to the seminary, but his successor refused

[59] *Schema B,* can. 297, n. 6—*Cadicis Iuris Canonici Schemata, Lib. IV De Processibus,* p. 436; *Schema D,* can. 428, n. 5—*ibid.; Schema E,* can. 449, n. 5—*ibid.,* p. 437; *Schema F,* can. 401, n. 5, ibid.; *Schema G.* can. 388, n. 3—*ibid.,* p. 435. There is a notation, however, to the last canon cited: "Cavendum est ne in hoc canone repetantur quae supra statuta sunt, praesertim in cap. *De actionibus ob nullitatem actorum.*" But there is no indication as to who is responsible for this reference to canons 1679-1680 of the Code.

[60] Cf. Roberti, "Codicis iuris canonici Schemata de processibus,"—*Acta Congressus Iuridici Internationalis 1934,* IV, 33.

[61] Cf. Serédi, "De valore iuridico fontium Codicis I. C.,"—*Jus Pontificium,* I (1921), 63-66; also *Proemium* to *Fontes,* I, v.

[62] *S. Iacobi de Chile, restitutionis in integrum et compromissi,* 5 iulii 1927, *coram R. P. D. Francisco Parrillo,* dec. XXXIV—*Decisiones,* XIX (1927), 276-298.

to recognize the oral contract. The case was tried by the archdiocesan court of Santiago and its decision against Zavala was confirmed by the appeal tribunal. Zavala then sought *restitutio in integrum* from the Rota. The *turnus* in nine pages of exposition of the law on the extraordinary remedy espoused D'Angelo's opinion and used many of his arguments verbatim in its support.[63]

In applying to the facts of the case the idea that *legis praescriptum* included procedural law, the Rota passed over the minor violations in the sentence of the appeal court which did not clearly demonstrate the injustice of the sentence; but these did, when added to another and graver violation, establish the fact of injustice with certainty. *Restitutio* was granted in virtue of canon 1905, § 2, 4°, because the promoter of justice was not present. At the first trial he was present but took no active part, excusing himself as a resident of the seminary and therefore prejudiced in the case. In the second trial he was neither cited nor present so that the appeal court also violated canon 1595, which demands that the appeal tribunal be constituted just as that of the first instance.[64]

In an earlier decision the Rota granted *restitutio,* without any discussion of the interpretation of *legis praescriptum,* because of a violation of the canons on contumacy, noting also that the promoter of justice had acted as procurator of the bishop in conjunction with his own office, contrary to canon 1613, § 2.[65] In other decisions petitions for *restitutio* in view of an infraction of procedural law have been denied, not because the Auditors did not accept this interpretation of the law, but because an evident violation was not demonstrated or some other condition was not fulfilled. In one case the remedy was refused because the petitioner was responsible for the damage he incurred by failing to appeal.[66]

[63] *Ibid.,* nn. 3-16; pp. 278-287.

[64] *Ibid,* nn. 17-21, pp. 287-289.

[65] *Incidentis super contumacia,* 24 iulii 1923, dec. XXI—*Decisiones,* XV (1923), 180-189.

[66] *Restitutionis in integrum, diffamationis,* 16 febr. 1925, dec. XI, nn. 2-3—*Decisiones* XVII (1925), 83-84; cf. also in an earlier hearing of the

Likewise in the year 1927 a petition was refused because what was claimed to be a violation of procedural law on the part of the judge was rather the neglecting of a particular law on the part of the petitioner; whereas the latter asserted that the judge did not try to have a case of diffamation settled amicably and hence violated canons 1925 and 1932, as a matter of fact the petitioner had refused to have the case arbitrated as the statutes of the university in which he was a professor demanded.[67] In a more recent case the remedy was refused because the asserted violations of canons 1835-1840 and of canon 1616 were not sufficiently demonstrated.[68] In this case the *turnus* refused to discuss the disputed interpretation of *legis praescriptum* because no violation was proved.[69]

The objection that D'Angelo's interpretation would allow the revocation of a sentence for the violation of minor requirements of procedural law is easily answered. *Restitutio in integrum* would never be granted because of a minor infraction of law, e. g., the omission of the name of the judge from the sentence contrary to canon 1874, § 2. *Restitutio* is to be given only to repair grave damage. The damage to be repaired by the remedy against the sentence is the injustice of the *res iudicata.* For the damage to be great the injustice must be great; for the injustice to be great because of a violation of the procedural law, it must be a serious infraction in a grave matter. *Causa causae est causa causati.* Grave damage sufficient for *restitutio in integrum* will not result for a minor violation of the law.

same case: "Neque in modum procedendi aliquid errore irrepsit"—17 ian. 1913, dec. II, n. 11—*Decisiones,* XV (1923), 16.

[67] *Restitutionis in integrum,* 29 martii 1927, dec. XII—*Decisiones,* XIX (1927), 92-98.

[68] *Poenarum. . . et restitutionis in integrum,* 31 iulii 1930, dec. LXIV, n. 13—*Decisiones,* XXII (1930), 501.

[69] *Ibid.,* n. 18, p. 504. Except for the Santiago decision of 1927, of which D'Angelo knew only from hearsay *(Periodica,* XVIII [1929], 61*), these Rota decisions which show an inclination toward his opinion were not cited by D'Angelo. All of them have been published only since his death in 1931.

Article IV. Conclusion

Because of this dispute as to which remedy—the plaint of nullity or *restitutio in integrum*—is intended to attack a sentence which has terminated a process in which the procedural law has been violated, a doubt of law exists. The prudent procurator and advocate will advise clients who find themselves damaged by such a violation to seek both remedies. A petition can be drawn up asking for a declaration of the nullity of the sentence or, if it is not null, a *restitutio*.[70] Until the jurisprudence of the higher tribunals is established by clear and repeated decisions or unless the Pontifical Commission for the Interpretation of the Code gives an authentic interpretation, a judge is free to accept either opinion.

Theoretically, however, it is the conclusion of the present writer that the opinion which includes in *legis praescriptum evidenter neglectum* the violation of formal procedural law is the better founded. This conclusion is based on the following considerations:

1) The arguments adduced to uphold the extensive interpretation of canons 1892 and 1894 are inconclusive.

2) The general term *legis praescriptum* can include any law. Hence violations of procedural law are not to be excluded on the ground that they cannot render a sentence unjust.

3) It is the common opinion. The bare numerical preponderance of writers in its favor means little; certainly the opinion of Roberti, doubtless the present outstanding authority on canonical procedure, and Hanssen, who has devoted serious study to the question, weighs more than the offhand assertion of many compendiarists who have written on the whole codification. Yet, such grave canonists as Vidal, Creusen, and Coronata, as well as Msgr. D'Angelo, have adhered to it after considering both views.

4) It clearly defines the province of the two remedies: *querela nullitatis* for the cases listed in canons 1892, 1894; *restitutio in*

[70] Cf. e. g., S. R. R., *Proprietatis,* 11 aug. 1930, dec. LII, n. 5—*Decisiones,* XXII (1930), 587.

integrum for grave damage resulting from the injustice of the *res iudicata* due to the neglect of any law. In the other opinion both remedies could be available at the same time since, as Hanssen admits, "the limits between substantive laws and formal ones are not always distinct." He moreover makes a remarkable concession to the opposing view: although *restitutio* is not to be granted for the violation of a formal law, it "should not be denied on the pretext that a merely formal law was neglected."[71]

5) It labors under no more difficulties than the opposite opinion.

6) It has the jurisprudence of the Roman tribunals more in its favor, as appears from the discussion in the previous article.

[71] "Restitutio in integrum concedenda est contra sententiam manifeste iniustam, qualis esse poterit, si evidenter neglecta fuerit lex substantialis, aut etiam lex processualis quae bona in processu distribuat, imo ne denegetur praetextu quod neglecta sit tantum lex formalis. Limites enim inter leges substantiales et formales non semper sunt distincti. Singuli casus considerentur; et si sententia, licet aliunde, videatur iniusta, nec suppetat remedium appellationis aut querelae, propter neglectum legis praescriptum facile concedatur restitutio in integrum."—*Apollinaris,* XII (1939), 248. Hanssen thus destroys the limitative force of canon 1905, § 2 when he allows *restitutio* if the sentence, *licet aliunde, videatur iniusta.* Canon 1905 allows the remedy if the injustice is manifest because of the violation of law; Hanssen allows it if the sentence is unjust, not because of the violation of a law, but for some other reason!

Chapter XI

THE CONCESSION OF THE REMEDY

Article I. The Competent Court

Canon 1906. Ad restitutionem in integrum concedendam competens est iudex qui sententiam tulit, nisi ea petatur ex neglecto a iudice praescripto legis; quo in casu eam concedit tribunal appellationis.

The competency to accept a petition for *restitutio in integrum* against a sentence which has become irrevocably adjüdged depends on the reason for which it is sought. If the reason is an error of fact—one of the causes listed in canon 1905, § 2, 1°, 2°, 3°—the court which pronounced the sentence is competent, and any superior court is absolutely incompetent. If the reason is an error of law—"the neglect of a prescript of law" in canon 1905, § 2, 4°—the petition must go to the court of appeal; the judge who pronounced the sentence is absolutely incompetent.[1]

The reason for establishing the superior court as the only competent one to consider sentences attacked as a result of the neglect of the law is that the judge who rendered the sentence has thereby brought himself under suspicion. If he neglected a law by violation or omission in one trial, he may do so again, whether the law he neglected was a substantive law or a formal one of procedure. Moreover, the legislator does not wish to constrain a judge to admit his own error by changing his decision; and to ask a judge to decide whether he has judged rightly is to make him judge in his own cause.[2]

In enunciating the principles on competency, canon 1906 speaks first of "judge" and then of "tribunal." As a remedy against the sentence *restitutio* may be asked against the sentence

[1] Cf. Roberti, *De Processibus,* II, 265; I, 112; S. R. Rota, *Poenarum . . . et restitutionis in integrum,* 30 iulii 1930, dec. XLIV, n. 11—*Decisiones,* XXII (1930), 501.

[2] Cf. Woywod, *Hom. Past. Rev.,* XXXIII, part 1 (1932-1933), 379; Wernz-Vidal, *Ius Canonicum,* VI, n. 640

either of a single judge or of a collegiate tribunal. Like an appeal, the petition for this remedy, it seems, should be considered by a single judge if the sentence attacked was rendered by one judge, and by a collegiate tribunal if the sentence emanated from such.[3] *Restitutio* against the sentence is a matter solely of jurisdiction, not involving administrative power.[4] For this reason it can be granted also by a delegated judge against his own sentence.[5] If the petition is to be made to the judge or tribunal which issued the sentence, the same persons, if convenient, should constitute the court.[6]

A. Error of fact. Although the canon makes a clear distinction as to the ground for the remedy, it makes none concerning the basis of the *res iudicata.* If the sentence attacked is a single one which has become irrevocably adjudged, either because of the failure to appeal or because no appeal was possible,[7] the solution is obvious. The court which passed the sentence is competent if the remedy is sought for an error of fact; the petition must go to the appeal court if it indicates an error of law.

What if the *res iudicata* rises from two conforming sentences?[8] Both the court of the first instance and that of the second are the *"iudex qui sententiam tulit."* There is no clear principle of law on which to base a conclusion as to which is competent to grant a *restitutio* for an error of fact. The opposing views of authors must stand solely on the reasons which they adduce. Muniz[9] and Wernz-Vidal[10] hold that the petition should be made to the judge of the first instance. He it was who passed

[3] Cf. canon 1595.

[4] Cf. Lega-Bartoccetti, *op. cit.,* I, 436.

[5] Cf. Roberti, *De Processibus,* II, 265-266; Coronata, *Institutiones,* III, n. 1428. The limitation of canon 1688, § 1, "from an ordinary judge," should not be applied to the remedy against the sentence because of the phrase "within the limits of canons 1687, 1688;" canon 1906 considers the competency of the judge independently of the earlier canons.

[6] Roberti, *De Processibus,* II. 265.

[7] Canons 1902, 2°-3°; 1880.

[8] Canon 1902, 1°.

[9] *Procedimientos Eclesiásticos,* III, n. 521.

[10] *Ius Canonicum,* VI, n. 640.

the sentence; the superior court has merely confirmed it. It was the first judge who changed the status of the petitioner and of the controversy; he should therefore make the restoration. And since the remedy paves the way for a new discussion of the case, this can be done better before the court of first instance; the parties should not be asked to recur with expense to an appeal court which is perhaps very distant. Roberti and others, however, maintain that the court of second instance is alone competent. The status of *res iudicata* formally proceeds from the second sentence. The appeal court can admit new proofs, according to canon 1891, § 2, which were unknown to the inferior judge. The reason for the *restitutio,* e. g., the fraud of one party, may occur only in the higher court; hence there is no reason for calling on the judge of the lower court.[11]

Since canon 1906 does not distinguish and since grave authors disagree, a doubt of law exists. In the face of this *dubium iuris* it cannot be said that either court would act invalidly in accepting and passing sentence on a petition for *restitutio* based on an error of fact. The opinion of Roberti, however, seems the better. The case has already been seen by the appeal court; the acts of the case are on file there. The difficulty placed on the parties in going to the higher tribunal cannot be pressed, since the same would be true in every case of appeal. The argument that the first court changed the status of the case and should therefore restore it would be equally effective in case of an error of law, and yet such a case is remanded to the court of appeal. Especially when false documents have been employed or the fraud of one party intervened in only the higher court it seems that that court alone is the one "who passed the sentence."

Restitutio in integrum against a rotal sentence for an error of fact can come only from the Signatura.[12]

B. Error of law. If *restitutio* "is sought for neglect of a pre-

[11] Roberti, *De Processibus,* II, 265; Coronata, *Institutiones,* III, n. 1428; Woywod, *Hom. Past. Rev.,* XXXIII, part 1 (1932-1933), 378-379; Lemieux, *The Sentence,* p. 102.

[12] Canon 1603, § 1, 3°.

script of the law by a judge," states canon 1906, "in that case the tribunal of appeal concedes it." Again the cause that constituted the *res iudicata* must be considered. It if rises from one sentence, the court of appeal will be the one usually invoked in the hierarchy of courts. The appeal court of a suffragan bishop is that of the metropolitan.[13] The case heard in first instance by a metropolitan court or by the court of a see immediately subject to the Holy See is remanded to that court which it has chosen, with the approval of the Holy See, for all appeal cases.[14]

The Sacred Roman Rota is an ordinary court of appeal for all inferior courts, so that a petition for this remedy can be made to it against the sentence of a judge of first instance, the mediate court of appeal being passed by.[15]

If the *res iudicata* results from conforming sentences of two different instances, the court of appeal will of necessity be a tribunal of the Holy See, as there is no court of third instance elsewhere.[16] The Rota is competent to judge a petition for *restitutio in integrum* against the sentence of an inferior court on the ground of canon 1905, § 2, 4°, and on that alone.[17] If the

[13] Canon 1594, § 1.

[14] Canon 1594, § 2, §3.

[15] Canon 1599, § 1, 1°; cf. Roberti, *De Processibus,* I, 214.

[16] The Madrid Rota formerly functioned similarly to the Roman Rota, but because of political conditions in Spain its privileges were suspended by Pius XI from August 1, 1933; cf. *Apollinaris,* VII (1934), 131.

[17] Cf. S. R. Rota, *Poenarum . . . et restitutionis in integrum,* 30 iulii 1930, dec. XLIV, n. 11—*Decisiones* XXII (1930), 501; *Corduben.,* 12 iulii 1929, dec. XXXII, n. 12—*Decisiones,* XXI (1929), 277. Woywod (*Hom. Past. Rev.,* XXXIII [1932-1933], 379) can find no competent court to receive the petition against the sentence of an appeal court for the violation of law because canon 1599, § 1, 1°-2°, makes the Rota competent in the second instance for an appeal and in higher instances only if the sentence has not become irrevocably adjudged. But canon 1906 by the phrase "tribunal of appeal" designates the tribunal to which an appeal would go if the sentence were not irrevocably adjudged; *restitutio* is not an appeal. In an early case the Rota found its competence in the *Lex Propria,* can. 14, § 4—*De Manila,* 18 febr. 1919—*AAS,* XII (1920), 186-187. In later cases, e. g., those cited at the beginning of this note, the Rota considered its competence as clearly stated in canon 1906.

petition is for a *restitutio* against a rotal sentence for an error of law, just as for an error of fact, the only competent court is the Apostolic Signatura.[18]

Article II. Procedure

Just as the Code sets up no specific norms of procedure for discussing *restitutio in integrum* as a general remedy, neither does it for the use of the remedy against the sentence.

The proceedings for *restitutio* against the sentence have two stages—one to determine whether the remedy is to be granted, the other to provide a new hearing on the merits of the case. Both should be carried out, but the party against whom the remedy is granted may acquiesce and renounce a further trial on the merits of the question. The practice of the Rota, however, is to try both questions conjointly, even though the parties may wish otherwise.[19] If the remedy is conceded by the Signatura against a rotal sentence, the case is returned to the Rota for the discussion as to its merits.[20] Otherwise the court which grants the remedy is the one to reconsider the question.

In the first stage of the discussion proofs must be presented to demonstrate that one of the conditions of canon 1905, § 2, is verified, so that the *res iudicata* is manifestly unjust; any one of these conditions constitutes the just cause needed for the extraordinary remedy. Further, it must be evident that an appeal or plaint of nullity is not possible and that the conditions of canons 1687 and 1688 are fulfilled. An adult therefore must show that he is not responsible for his plight.[21] It should be determined that the four years allowed by canon 1688, § 1, have not elapsed. The quadriennium begins for minors with the attainment of their majority; for adults it ordinarily begins when the sentence becomes a *res iudicata*. But if the remedy is sought

[18] Canon 1603, § 1, 4°.

[19] *Corduben.*, 12 iulii 1929, dec. XXXII, nn. 12, 14—*Decisiones,* XXI (1929) 278-279.

[20] Canon 1604, § 3.

[21] Canon 1688, § 2.

for an error of fact, the time does not begin to run until the person aggrieved by the sentence becomes aware of the error by the discovery of new documents or by learning that the sentence was based on false ones or procured through the fraud of the other party. Until then he is impeded.[22] If the remedy is sought in view of an error of law, the time should be computed from the day on which the sentence became irrevocably adjudged.[23] The quadriennium is computed as for the remedy in general; it is in the nature of usable time both in its beginning and in its course.[24]

For the process a procurator, just as for the remedy against any other act, needs a special mandate.[25] The promoter of justice should be cited in every case of *restitutio in integrum* against the sentence to protect the status of the *res iudicata,*[26] although if he is not present the acts of the case will not be invalid.

In the second stage of the process—that concerning the merits of the case—new proofs can be presented in addition to the ones of the original trial. Roberti allows the presentation of new proofs when the remedy is given for an error of fact but not when it is granted because of the neglect of a law.[27] This is consistent with his interpretation of canon 1905, § 2, 4°; if the neglect of a prescript of the law extends only to the substantive law, there is no need for admitting new proofs; all the judge need do is reconsider the facts presented in the proper setting of law and render his decision. But since *legis praescriptum*

[22] Roberti, *De Processibus,* II, 267.

[23] Wernz-Vidal, *Ius Canonicum.* VI, n, 641; Muniz, *Procedimientos Eclesiásticos,* III, n. 522; Roberti counts the time from the notification of the sentence—*De Processibus,* II, 267.

[24] Cf. *supra,* The Rota once, contrary to the interpretation of the authors, said the time should be computed from the execution of the sentence, no matter how much later this occurred, rather than from the time when the sentence became irrevocably adjudged, because the damage occurred only then.—*De Manila,* 18 febr. 1919—*AAS,* XII (1920), 190.

[25] Cf. Coronata, *Institutiones,* III, n. 1426; Roberti, *De Processibus,* II, 266.

[26] Muniz, *Procedimientos Eclesiasticos,* III, n. 522; Roberti, *De Processibus,* I, 197; Glynn, *The Promoter of Justice,* p. 318.

[27] *De Processibus,* II, 268.

more probably connotes also the procedural law, the permission of new proofs will frequently be imperative. For example, if canon 1861, § 2, were violated by the admission of new proofs without the knowledge of the other party, the petitioner should be allowed to present proofs to the contrary.[28] Or if unsworn witnesses were accepted in violation of canon 1767, § 1, in justice to the party who presented them, the same or new witnesses, duly sworn, should be heard; of if the promoter of justice was absent when his presence was required according to canon 1587, in the new trial he should have the right to present proof.

Article III. Effects

Canon 1907.—§ 1. Petitio restitutionis in integrum sententiae exsecutionem nondum inceptam suspendit.

§ 2. Si tamen suspicio sit ex probabilibus indiciis petitionem factam esse ad moras exsecutioni nectendas, iudex decernere potest ut sententia exsecutioni demandetur, assignata tamen restitutionem petenti idonea cautione ut, si restituatur in integrum, indemnis fiat.

The petition for *restitutio* and the concession of it have separate effects. Canon 1907 provides only for those of the petition for the remedy. A petition for *restitutio in integrum* suspends the execution of the sentence which has not yet been commenced. If the execution has been begun in any way, it need not be held up because one of the parties to the case seeks the remedy.[29] The provision of canon 1907, § 1, is a precaution against a futile execution of the sentence which, even though it has become irrevocably adjudged and should therefore be executed,[30] may nevertheless be revoked by *restitutio*.

In canon 1907, § 2, the law provides, however, for the execution of the sentence if it appears that the remedy is sought only for the sake of delay. In order to do this, the judge must have a well founded suspicion—*ex probabilibus indiciis*— as to the

[28] Cf. Roberti, *De Processibus,* II, 161.
[29] Vermeersch-Creusen, *Epitome,* III, n. 246.
[30] Canon 1917, § 1.

motives of the petitioner. The execution is to be merely a provisory one depending on the outcome of the further examination of the case. Hence the person in whose favor it is made is required to put up a guaranty—*idonea cautione*—that he will restore everything as it should be if the *restitutio* is granted.[31] The words of canon 1907, § 1, which allow the execution of the sentence because of a suspicion that the petitioner has no real case are not preceptive; the judge may—*potest*—order the provisory execution; if he does, the guaranty must be given. It can be verbal, like a promise, or something more tangible, which is actually handed over to the judge or to the other party, e. g., a note or a bond.[32] The indemnity which the canon assures to the petitioner if he receives the *restitutio* is not only to cover the principal object of the suit but also any interest or loss of profit sustained in the interim.[33]

The chief effect of the concession of *restitutio in integrum* against the sentence is like that of any grant of this remedy—a complete restoration to previous condition. The *res iudicata* and the sentence or sentences on which it was based are swept away. A new sentence decides the merits of the case and it is usually unique. It can therefore be attacked by all possible remedies, including *restitutio in integrum.* Even if it conforms with the sentence which preceded the *restitutio,* it is presumed to have a new motivation either of fact or of law.[34] This is certainly true if the *res iudicata* resulted from one sentence or if in case of two conforming sentences, both have been found unjust according to canon 1905, § 2.

What if the unjust *res iudicata* was based on two conforming sentences and only one of these can be attacked because of one of the grounds listed in canon 1905, § 2? If the second sentence is found to be unjust for any error of fact or of law which

[31] Cf. c. 6, X, *de in integrum restitutione,* I, 41.

[32] Blat, *De Processibus,* n. 440.

[33] Blat, *loc. cit.;* Cappello, *Summa Iuris Canonici,* III, n. 364.

[34] Cf. Roberti, *De Processibus,* II, 268; Coronata, *Institutiones,* III, n. 1429.

did not also occur in the first trial, the sentence of the first instance remains firm. The status of the case will depend on the decision as to the merits of the case rendered after the *restitutio.* If the new sentence confirms the first, a new *res iudicata* arises; if it reforms the first sentence, two non-conforming sentences exist and appeal is possible within ten days.

Is it possible in view of an error of fact or of law to impugn the injustice of the first of two conforming sentences when such an error has not reoccurred in the second trial? Each one of the circumstances listed in canon 1905, § 2, must be considered separately. The discovery of new documents after the *res iudicata* comes into being can be a ground only for attacking either the second or both sentences. If the first sentence were based on false documents or procured through the fraud of one party and the second decision was not, *restitutio* should not, it seems, be conceded. The remedy is allowed because of injustice resulting from the sentence being based on a false foundation of facts. If the appeal court has arrived at the same conclusion as the lower court without recurring to the false documents or devices of one party, it appears that there would have been sufficient motivation for the first sentence even if the false proofs or fraud had not been employed.

If a law was neglected in the first court and not in the second, the same conclusion, it seems, should be drawn. The fact that the decision of the court of appeal concurred with the earlier sentence destroys the presumption that the violation of law engendered grave injustice to the petitioner's rights. These distinctions are offered, *salvo meliori iudicio,* in the silence of the authors on the problem. Only Muniz hints at an opposite solution when he states, in speaking of the competency of various courts, that, if a law were neglected in the first instance and not in the second, the case for *restitutio* must go to a yet higher tribunal; the reason is, he says, that though the second court did not itself violate the law, it should have perceived the neglect of law in the acts of the first process and is therefore likewise suspect.[35]

[35] *Procedimientos Eclesiásticos,* III, n. 521.

If the original sentence has already been executed, anything which has changed hands through the execution is to be restored if the sentence passed after the *restitutio in integrum* reverses the original decision.[36]

Article IV. Two Corollaries

A. The Criminal Sentence

Is *restitutio in integrum* available to revoke the sentence rendered in a criminal trial? Many writers before the Code answered negatively.[37] Yet some considered it a possible remedy.[38] In the law of the Code the sentence terminating a criminal process becomes a *res iudicata,* because the law makes no exception for it. [39] There are no special norms laid down in Section II of the Fourth Book of the Code on remedies against the criminal sentence. Canon 1959 merely states that with the execption of the rules prescribed in the preceding canons the norms of the first section of Book IV on civil cases are to be applied. Given,

[36] Roberti, *De Processibus,* II, 264. Eichmann considers the effect of a granted *restitutio* to be merely the quashing of the *res iudicata* so that the sentence must be attacked by an appeal or plaint of nullity: ". . . dass der Zustand wiederhergestellt wird, welcher vor dem Eintritt der Rechtskraft des Urteils bestanden hatte; das Urteil kann also jetzt mit den ordentlichen Rechtsmitteln (Berufung, Nichtigkeitsbeschwerde) angefochten werden."—*op. cit.,* p. 187. But according to canon 1905 *restitutio* is used "adversus sententiam" and not against the status of *res iudicata;* the effect of *restitutio* is always to treat as not existing that which it revokes; cf. c. 4, X, *de in integrum restitutione,* I, 41.

[37] Cf. Schmalzgrueber, *op. cit.,* I tit. 41, n. 2; Bouix, *De Iudiciis,* II, 404, 412; Droste-Messmer, *Canonical Procedure in Disciplinary and Criminal Cases of Clerics* (New York, 1897), n. 113; Lega, *Praelectiones . . . de Iudiciis Ecclesiasticis* (4 vols., Romae, 1896-1901), IV, n. 363; Smith said it could be granted, but only by the Holy See—*The New Procedure in Criminal and Disciplinary Causes of Ecclesiastics in the United States* (3. ed., New York, 1890), n. 573.

[38] Cf. Wernz, *Ius Decretalium,* V, 556; Heiner, *De Processu Criminali Ecclesiastico* (translated by Arthur Wynen, Romae, 1912), p. 137; Hergenröther, *Lehrbuch des katholischen Kirchenrechts* (2. ed., by Joseph Hollweck, Freiburg im Breisgau, 1905), n. 783.

[39] Cf. Muniz, *Procedimientos Eclesiásticos,* III, n. 637, note 1.

then, all of the conditions required by canon 1905, *restitutio* should be available to attack a criminal sentence.

Though many writers since the Code are silent on the point, all those who consider the question allow *restitutio* in favor of a person condemned by a criminal sentence. And the Rota has, as a matter of fact, considered petitions for *restitutio in integrum* against condemnatory sentences rendered in criminal processes.[40] But all of the writers approach the question from the point of view of the condemned party. If a sentence condemning the accused is unjust, it should be revoked by the extraordinary remedy.[41] What if the sentence absolved the accused person? Could the promoter of justice attack it with a petition for *restitutio in integrum?* The law is silent. So too are the commentators. The question can be answered only by applying to it the principles on the extraordinary remedy.

The promoter of justice is the plaintiff in the criminal case [42] If he loses his case, he should be armed with all remedies against the sentence which any other plaintiff would have. The injustice of the *res iudicata* is manifest if one of the circumstances of canon 1905, § 2, is demonstrated. The injustice is the damage to be repaired by *restitutio.* But here is the core of the problem. Can the injustice of the sentence be construed as grave damage

[40] *Restitutionis in integrum, diffamationis,* 19 ian. 1923, dec. II—*Decisiones,* XV (1923), 9-17; a later hearing of the same case: *Luganen,* 16 febr. 1925, dec. XI—*Decisiones,* XVII (1925), 81-90.

[41] De Meester, *Juris Canonici et Juris Canonico-Civilis Compendium* (Brugis: Desclée de Brouwer, 1921-1928), III, pars II, n. 1610, note 4; Muniz, *Procedimientos Eclesiásticos,* III, n. 637; Coronata, *Institutiones,* III, n. 1476; *idem, Manuale Practicum Iuris Disciplinaris et Criminalis Regularium* (Taurini: Marietti, 1938), nn. 228-231; Ranier, *The Suspension of Clerics,* Catholic University of America Canon Law Studies, n. 111, (Washington: Catholic University, 1937), p. 183. Of the authors cited Coronata alone can be said not to refer only to a condemnatory sentence as clearly as the others; in the *Manuale Practicum* he merely includes a treatment on the remedy along with other parts of the general norms on procedure, which he has collected as applicable to the criminal process; in the *Institutiones* he only remarks in a footnote the possibility of the remedy.

[42] Cf. canon 1934; Blat, *De Processibus,* n. 509; Glynn, *The Promoter of Justice,* pp. 96 ff.

to the promoter of justice? Certainly the public good, or even the Church, may be said to suffer damage if a crime goes unpunished. But the promoter suffers no damage. In the criminal case he is the prosecutor and though he represents the Church, he is not the Church; the intangible damage which the Church suffers is not personal. There is lacking the *interesse* which has always been the reason behind a concession of the extraordinary remedy.

In Roman law a minor could not receive a *restitutio in integrum* for a criminal prosecution which he had omitted at the proper time.[43] Reiffenstuel gave as the reason for this that it did not pertain to his patrimonial affairs but rather to the meting out of punishment.[44] Durantis likewise denied the possibility of the Church invoking *restitutio* to present an exception because of a committed crime after the lapse of the proper time. He was writing of a case concerning the possession of a benefice, but his arguments were general: The aid of *restitutio* was not prepared for the execution of penalties; the church loses nothing by not being able to propose the crime; the church feels no financial loss, and any damage sustained by the public good because of a crime going unpunished is not the type of damage to be considered for this remedy.[45] Likewise Pirhing argued that the church could not receive a *restitutio in integrum* against the lapse of time to present proof in a criminal trial, for the church in such a case suffered no pecuniary damage.[46]

Restitutio was introduced into the law because of natural equity to assist minors primarily and also others who find themselves

[43] D. (4, 4) 37, pr.

[44] "quia huiusmodi res non ad rem familiarem, sed potius ad ultionem pertinet"—*op. cit.,* I, tit. 41, n. 104.

[45] "Nam in executionibus poenarum non est paratum auxilium restitutionis . . . nam ibi ecclesia nihil de suo iure non proponendo deperiret, nec illi aliquid accresceret proponendo . . . nil incommodi pecuniarii sentit, de quo interesse iura curaverunt, non autem de publico interesse, de quo dicitur, quod publicae utilitatis est, ne crimina remaneant impunita. . ."—*Speculum Iuris,* lib. II, partic. III, *h. t.,* § II, n. 8.

[46] *Ius Canonicum,* I, tit. 41, n. 21; cf. also Panormitanus, *Commentaria,* I, h. t., c. 3, n. 16.

gravely damaged and bereft of any other remedy. It was not intended as a lengthening of the arm of law enforcement. The canonical jurisprudence has been constantly opposed, as has been noted, to the use of *restitutio in integrum* as a means of prosecuting crime, because the type of damage for which the remedy is intended does not exist in the case wherein the church finds itself unable further to prosecute a criminal.

In the silence of all other writers, then, with due regard for a better judgment it is here held that *restitutio in integrum* is possible in favor of the accused party who has been condemned by a sentence which is irrevocably adjudged; it is not available to the promoter of justice to reopen an irrevocably adjudged case in which the accused has been acquitted.

B. Restoration to Appeal

It was clear in the old law that *restitutio* was available against the *fatalia* allowed for an appeal; this remedy did not revoke the existing sentence but merely restored to the petitioner another period of ten days in which he could appeal from it. It was quite distinct from a *restitutio* against three conforming sentences.[47] A similar provision is made in the present law to allow a contumacious party to regain the right to appeal through a *restitutio in integrum* without revoking the sentence.[48] Beyond this case, of which the law makes particular mention, any restoration against the lapse of time which results in the sentence becoming irrevocably adjudged has been abolished by the Code.

If a person fails to appeal in ten days, the sentence becomes irrevocably adjudged and cannot be appealed.[49] Canon 1905 allows a *restitutio in integrum* against an unappealable sentence only if the sentence is manifestly unjust in one of the ways definitely and exhaustively determined in that canon. No ex-

[47] Cf. c. un., *de restitutione in integrum,* I, 11, in Clem; Hostiensis, *Summa Aurea,* I. h. t., n. 9: Reiffenstuel, *op. cit.,* I, tit. 41, n. 80; De Luca, *De Iudiciis,* disc. 37, n. 19.

[48] Canon 1847.

[49] Canons 1902, 2°; 1880, 4°.

ception is made for the manner in which the sentence became a *res iudicata.*[50]

Besson, however, argues that in spite of the apparent general terms of canon 1905, the distinction of the old law is still in force. The conditions of canon 1905, he maintains, are applicable only when *restitutio* is sought directly against the sentence itself, not when it is sought directly against the lapse of time and only indirectly against the sentence.[51] He bases this distinction on the practice of the Rota from which he cites two decisions. One of these was prior to the Code.[52] The other was a rehearing of a case which had been decided before 1918; the *turnus* had to decide whether the pre-Code law had been properly applied by the earlier judges.[53] Several years later, however, the Rota again discussed the distinction between the two types of *restitutio,* that to appeal and that against the sentence. Though the Rota quoted a pre-Code decision and praised it for granting the remedy to appeal, the *turnus* actually granted the remedy on the grounds of canon 1905, § 2, 4°.[54] In the same year the Rota tried a petition for *restitutio* against a sentence which was irrevocably adjudged in view of the failure to appeal; the auditors applied canon 1905 to the case.[55]

In the present law, then, there is no longer possible any restoration against the lapse of time if the status of *res iudicata* has intervened. This applies not only to the lapse of the ten days to appeal, but also to the lapse of the month for beginning the prosecution of the appeal and the lapse of a year without some

[50] Cf. S. R. Rota, *Luganen.,* 16 febr., dec. XI, n. 2—*Decisiones,* XVII (1925), 82.

[51] "Sur la Restitution 'in integrum'," *Nouvelle Revue Théologique,* XLIV (1920), 463-475; cf. especially pp. 469, 471.

[52] *Novarien.,* 7 aug. 1917—*AAS,* X (1918), 336-343.

[53] *De Manila,* 18 febr. 1919—*AAS,* XII (1920), 183-200; the decision which it confirmed is found in *AAS,* VIII (1916), 275-288.

[54] *Incidentis super contumacia,* 24 iulii 1923, dec. XXI—*Decisiones,* XV (1923), 180-189.

[55] *Restitutionis in integrum, diffamationis,* 19 ian. 1923, dec. II—*Decisiones,* XV (1923), 9-17.

processual act being performed in the higher tribunal.[56] Those writers who speak of the use of the extraordinary remedy against the *fatalia appellationis* must be understood as confining that use within the limits indicated by canon 1905.[57] Such a restoration to appeal would in reality be useless. If one of the circumstances of 1905, § 2, is verified, then the sentence itself—all other conditions being fulfilled—can be revoked by the extraordinary remedy; it would be futile for anyone to ask merely for a restoration to appeal when he could use *restitutio* to obtain relief from the sentence itself.

[56] Cf. canons 1883, 1736.

[57] Cf. Noval, *De Iudiciis,* n. 343; Lega-Bartoccetti, *op. cit.,* I, 438. Since Lega requires the conditions of canon 1905 to be verified for a contumacious party to appeal in virtue of canon 1847 (*ibid.,* II, 876), he would certainly demand the same in other cases.

CONCLUSIONS

Gathered here in summary are the more important particular conclusions arrived at in this study on *restitutio in integrum.* Some are attempts to answer questions not raised by the authors of general works on canonical procedure. Others are what appear on the basis of new considerations to be the better of the contrary opinions offered on disputed points.

I. As to the remedy in general:

1. *Restitutio in integrum* can be invoked to rescind a contract even in countries where the civil law does not recognize this remedy.

2. Because in the matter of contracts the civil law of the region is to be followed, unless it is contrary to the divine law or unless the canon law provides otherwise, *restitutio* cannot ordinarily be used to revoke a contract which is null because it does not meet the civil law requirements.

3. The right to seek this remedy passes to the heirs and successors of minors and of persons, physical or moral, who enjoy their privileges; it does not pass to the heirs and successors of adults.

4. *Restitutio in integrum* is not available to attack a completed prescription unless the civil law of the place recognizes it as a remedy against prescription.

5. Though it is desirable that the promoter of justice be present at a hearing for the concession of *restitutio* when it is sought by minors or ecclesiastical moral persons, his presence is needed for the validity of the proceedings only when the remedy is given *ex officio.*

6. The provision of canon 1689 to protect the rights acquired in good faith by a third party before a petition is made for *restitutio* includes not only the right to the acquired fruits but also to the object itself if it has been acquired in good faith.

II. As to the remedy against the sentence:

7. Minors cannot use *restitutio in integrum* as a remedy against the sentence if an appeal or plaint of nullity is possible.

8. Outside of the case of a contumacious party, as specifically determined in canon 1847, *restitutio* against the lapse of any *fatalia* which have resulted in the sentence becoming irrevocably adjudged can be granted only according to the requirements of canon 1905.

9. The right to seek *restitutio in integrum* is not to be considered renounced when an appeal is renounced in writing.

10. Though *restitutio* cannot be used against a definitive sentence which does not become irrevocably adjudged, it can be used in cases concerning the status of persons against judicial acts, interlocutory sentences, or decrees.

11. The phrase *legis praescriptum* of canon 1905, § 2, 4°, is to be interpreted according to the common and extensive interpretation. It applies to formal procedural law as well as to substantive law, so that *restitutio in integrum* can be invoked to attack a sentence which is irrevocably adjudged if there was a grave violation of procedural law in the trial.

12. *Restitutio* can be granted to the *reus* to attack a condemnatory sentence which has become a *res iudicata* after a criminal process; but the promoter of justice cannot invoke it against a sentence which absolved the accused person.

BIBLIOGRAPHY

Sources

Acta Apostolicae Sedis, Commentarium Officiale, Romae, 1909—

Acta Gregorii Papae XVI, 4 vols., Romae, 1904.

Acta Sanctae Sedis, 41 vols., Romae, 1865-1908.

Antiquae Collectiones Decretalium cum Antonii Augustini Episcopi Ilerdensis notis, Illerdae, 1576.

Bruns, Herm., Theod., *Canones Apostolorum et Conciliorum saeculorum IV-V-VI-VII,* 2 vols., Berolini, 1839.

Bullarium Romanum, 24 vols. and supplement, Augustae Taurinorum, 1857-1872.

Bullarii Romani Continuatio Summorum Pontificum, 19 vols., Prato, 1756-1883.

Canones et Decreta Concilii Tridentini, Romae, 1845.

Codex Iuris Canonici, Pii X Pontificis Maximi iussu digestus, Benedicti Papae XV auctoritate promulgatus, Romae, 1917.

Codicis Iuris Canonici Fontes, cura Emi. Petri Card. Gasparri editi, vols. 1-6, Romae, 1922-1932; cura Emi. Iustiniani Card, Serédi, vols. 7-9, Romae, 1935-1939.

Codicis Iuris Canonici Schemata, Lib. IV De Processibus, I, De Iudiciis in Genere, digessit Franciscus Roberti, Civitate Vaticana: Typis Polyglottis Vaticanis-Pont. Inst. Utriusque Iuris, 1940.

Collectanea in usum Secretariae Sacrae Congregationis Episcoporum et Regularium, cura A. Bizzarii, secretarii, 2 ed. Romae, 1885.

Corpus Iuris Canonici, editio Lipsiensis post Iusti Henningii Boehmeri curas . . . denuo edidit Aemilius Ludovicus Richter, 2 vols., Lipsiae, 1839.

Corpus Iuris Civilis (Krueger-Mommsen-Schoell-Kroll), 3 vols., Berolini, 1928-1929.

Corpus Scriptorum Ecclesiasticorum Latinorum, ed. consilio et impensis Academiae Litterarum Caesareae Vindobonensis, Vindobonae, 1865—

Didascalia et Constitutiones Apostolorum, ed. F. X. Funk, 2 vols., Paderbornae, 1905.

Harduin, Jean, *Acta Conciliorum et Epistolae Decretales ac Constitutiones Summorum Pontificum,* 12 vols., Parisiis, 1715.

Hinschius, Paulus, *Decretales Pseudo-Isidorianae et Capitula Angilramni* Lipsiae, 1863.

Jaffé, Phillipus, *Regesta Pontificum Romanorum ab condita ecclesia ad annum post Christum natum MCXCVIII* 2. ed., 2 vols., Lipsiae, 1881-1888.

Lex Romana Canonice Compta, Testo di leggi romano-canoniche del sec. IX, ed. Carlo Guido Mor, Pavia: Tipografia Cooperativa, 1927.

Lex Romana Visigothorum, ed. Gustavus Haenel, Berolini, 1849.

Mansi, J. D., *Sacrorum Conciliorum Nova et Amplissima Collectio,* 53 vols., Parisiis, 1901-1927.

Migne, P. J., *Patrologiae Cursus Completus, Series Latina,* 221 vols., Parisiis, 1844-1855.

Monumenta Germaniae Historica, Epistolae Selectae, Tom. II, *Das Register Gregors VII,* 2 fasc., ed. Erich Casper, Berolini: apud Weidmannos, 1920-1925.

Monumenta Germaniae Historica, Epistolae, Tom. II, *Gregorii I Papae Registrum Epistolarum,* 2 parts, ed. Paulus Ewald et Ludovicus M. Hartmann, Berolini, 1891-1899.

Pallottini, Salvator, *Collectio Omnium Conclusionum et Resolutionum Congregationis Concilii ab anno 1564 ad annum 1860,* 17 vols., Romae, 1868-1895.

Quinta Compilatio Epistolarum Decretalium Honorii III Pont. Max., ed. Innocentius Cironius, Tolosae, 1645.

S. Romanae Rotae Decisiones seu Sententiae, Romae, 1912—; *Decisiones Recentiores,* 19 parts in 25 vols., Francofurti-Aureliae-Romae, 1623-1703.

Theodosiani Libri XVI cum Constitutionibus Sirmondianis, ediderunt Th. Mommsen et Paulus M. Meyer, 3 vols., Berolini, 1905.

Thesaurus Resolutionum Sacrae Congregationis Concilii, 167 vols., Romae, 1718-1908.

Authors

Acta Congressus Iuridici Internationalis Romae 12-17 novembris 1934, 5 vols., Romae: Pont. Inst. Utriusque Iuris, 1935-1937.

Arangio-Ruiz, Vincenzo, *Istituzioni di Diritto Romano,* Neapoli: Nicola Jovene, 1927.

Augustine [Bachofen], Charles, *A Commentary on Canon Law,* Vol. VII, *Ecclesiastical Trials,* 3 ed., St. Louis: Herder, 1930.

Barbosa, Augustinus, *Collectanea doctorum tam veterum quam recentiorum in ius pontificium universum,* 5 vols., Lugduni, 1656; *Tractatus Varii,* Lugduni, 1660.

Bartoccetti, Vittorio, *Le Regole Canoniche de Diritto in Relazione al Codice Piano-Benedettino,* Romae: Instituto Grafico Tiberino, 1939.

Bassibey, R., *Le Mariage devant les Tribunaux Ecclésiastiques, Procédure Matrimontale Générale,* Paris-Poitiers, 1899.

Bernardus Papiensis, *Summa Decretalium,* ed. E. A. Th. Laspeyres, Ratisbonae, 1860.

Biondi, Biondo, *Appunti intorno alla Sentenza nel Processo Civile Romano,* Pavia: Successori Fratelli Fusi, 1929.

Blat, Albertus, *Commentarium Textus Codicis Iuris Canonici, Liber IV, De Processibus,* Romae: Collegio Angelico, 1927.

Böckn, Placidus, *Commentarium in Ius Canonicum Universum,* 3 vols., Salisburgae, 1776.

Boich, Henricus, *In Quinque Decretalium Libros Commentaria,* 2 vols., Venetiis, 1576.

Bonfante, Pietro, *Storia del Diritto Romano,* 3. ed., 2 vols., Milano: Societa Editrice Libraria, 1923.

Bouix, D., *Tractatus de Iudiciis Ecclesiasticis,* 2. ed., 2 vols., Parisiis, 1855.

Buckland, W. W., *The Roman Law of Slavery,* Cambridge, 1908.

————, *A Text Book of Roman Law from Augustus to Justinian,* 2. ed., Cambridge: University Press, 1932.

Cala, Caesar, *Tractatus Absolutissimus de Feriis,* Neapoli, 1675.

Cappello, Felix M., *Summa Iuris Canonici,* 3 vols., Romae: Universitas Gregoriana, I-II, 3 ed., 1938-1939; III, 1936.

Cicognani, Amleto Giovanni, *Canon Law,* authorized English version by J. O'Hara and F. Brennan, 2. ed., Philadelphia: Dolphin Press, 1935.

Cleary, Joseph F., *Canonical Limitations on the Alienation of Church Property,* Catholic University of America Canon Law Studies, n. 100, Washington: Catholic University, 1936.

Cocchi, Guidus, *Commentarium in Codicem Iuris Canonici,* VII, *De Processibus,* 3. ed., Taurinorum Augustae: Marietti, 1940.

Connolly, Thomas A., *Appeals,* Catholic University of America Canon Law Studies, n. 79, Washington: Catholic University, 1932.

Coronata, Matthaeus Conte a, *Institutiones Iuris Canonici,* III, *De Processibus,* Taurini: Marietti, 1933; I, 2. ed., Taurini: Marietti, 1939.

————, *Manuale Practicum Iuris Disciplinaris et Criminalis Regularium,* Taurini: Marietti, 1938.

————, *Ius Publicum Ecclesiasticum,* 2. ed., Taurini: Marietti, 1934.

Costa, Emilio, *Profilo Storico del Processo Civile Romano,* Roma, 1918.

————, *Storia del Diritto Romano Privato dalle origini alle compilazioni giustinianee,* Torino: Fratelli Bocca, 1925.

Covarruvias y Leyva, Didacus, *Opera Omnia,* 2 vols., Antverpiae, 1638.

Cuq, Edouard, *Les Institutions Juridiques des Romains,* 2 vols., Paris, 1891-1902.

D'Angelo, Sosio, *Saggi su questioni giuridiche,* Torino: Lega Italiana Cattolica Editrice, 1928.

De Angelis, F., *Praelectiones Iuris Canonici ad methodum Decretalium Gregorii IX exactae,* 4 vols., Romae, 1877-1887.

De Francisi, Pietro, *Per la storia dell' Episcopalis Audientia fino alla Nov. XXXV (XXXIV) di Valentiniano,* Romae, 1915.

De Luca, Ioannes Baptista, *Theatrum Veritatis et Iustitiae,* 16 vols., Coloniae Agrippinae, 1706.

De Meester, A., *Juris Canonici et Juris Canonico-Civilis Compendium,* 2. ed., 3 vols. in 4, Brugis: Desclée de Brouwer, 1921-1928.

Devoti, Ioannes, *Institutiones Canonicae libri IV,* 2 vols., after the 4. Roman ed., Leodii, 1871.

Dolan, John Leo, *The Defendsor Vinculi, His Rights and Duties,* Catholic University of America Canon Law Studies, n. 85, Washington: Catholic University, 1934.

Droste, Francis, *Canonical Procedure in Disciplinary and Criminal Cases of Clerics,* ed. by Sebastian G. Messmer, New York, 1897.

Durandus [Durantis], Guglielmus, *Speculum Iuris,* 3 vols., Venetiis, 1577.

Eichmann, Eduard, *Das Prozessrecht des Codex Iuris Canonici,* Pader born: Schöningh, 1921.

Engel, Ludovicus, *Collegium Universi Iuris Canonici,* 9. ed., Beneventi, 1760.

Englemann, Arthur, and Millar, Robert Wyness, *A History of Continental Civil Procedure,* Boston: Little, Brown, and Company, 1927.

Fagnanus, Prosper, *Commentaria Decretalium,* 6 vols., Romae, 1661.

Ferreres, Ioannes B., *Institutiones Canonicae iuxta novissimum Codicem Pii X,* 2. ed., 2 vols., *Barcinone*: Eugenio Subirana, 1920.

Fournier, Paul, *Les Officialites au Moyen Age,* Paris, 1880.

——————, *Les Collections Canoniques attribuees a Yves de Chartres,* Paris, 1897.

——————, and Le Bras, Gabriel, *Histoire des Collections Canoniques en Occident depuis les fausses decretales jusqu'au décret de Gratien,* 2 vols., Paris: Recueil Sirey, 1931-1932.

Gillet, Pierre, *La Personnalité Juridique en Droit Ecclésiastique,* Malines: W. Godene, 1927.

Girard, Paul, *Manuel Elémentaire de Droit Romain,* 7. ed., Paris: Arthur Rousseau, 1924.

——————, *Mélanges de Droit Romain, I, Histoire des Sources,* Paris, 1912.

Gonzalez-Tellez, Emmanuel, *Commentaria Perpetua in singulos textus quinque librorum Decretalium Gregorii IX,* 5 vols., Venetiis, 1699.

Haring, Johann B., *Grundzüge des katholischen Kirchenrechts,* 3 ed., 2 vols., Graz: Ulrich Mosers, 1924.

Hefele, Charles Joseph, and Leclercq, H., *Histoire des Conciles,* 10 vols. in 19, Paris: Letouzey et Ane, 1907-1938.

Heiner, Franciscus, *De Processu Criminali Eccesliastico,* translated by Arthur Wynen, Romae, 1912.

Hergenröther, Philipp, *Lehrbuch des katholischen Kirchenrechts,* 2. ed. by Joseph Hollweck, Freiburg in Breisgau, 1905.

Hostiensis (Henricus de Segusio), *Summa Aurea,* Venetiis, 1570.

——————, *In Quinque libros Decretalium Commentaria,* 5 vols., Venetiis, 1581.

Jolowicz, H. F., *An Historical Introduction to the Study of Roman Law.* Cambridge: University Press, 1932.

Jovius, Alexander, *De Solemnitatibus in Contractibus Minorum,* Parmae, 1715.

Koeniger, Albert M., *Katholisches Kirchenrecht,* Freiburg im Breisgau: Herder, 1926.

Kuttner, Stephan, *Repertorium der Kanonistik* (1140-1234)—*Prodromus Corporis Glossarum,* I, Studi e Testi, n. 71, Citta del Vaticano: Biblioteca Apostolica Vaticana, 1937.

Laurin, Franciscus, *Introductio in Corpus Iuris Canonici,* Friburgi Brisgoviae, 1889.

Lega, Michael, *Praelectiones De Iudiciis Ecclesiasticis,* 4 vols., Romae, 1896-1901; Vol. I, 3. ed., Romae, 1905.

————, *Commentarius in Iudicia Ecclesiastica iuxta Codicem Iuris Canonici,* curante Victorio Bartoccetti, 2 vols., Romae: Anonima Libraria Cattolica Italiana, 1938-1939.

Lemieux, Delisle Antoine, *The Sentence in Ecclesiastical Procedure,* Catholic University of America Canon Law Studies, n. 87, Washington: Catholic University, 1934.

Leurenius, Petrus, *Forum Ecclesiasticum in quo Ius Canonicum Universum explanatur,* 5 vols. in 3, Venetiis, 1729.

Lijdsman, Bernardus, *Introductio in Jus Canonicum cum uberiori fontium studio,* 2 vols., Hilversum in Hollandia; Societas Editrix Pontificia Anonyma, 1924-1929.

Michiels, Gommarus, *Principia Generalia de Personis in Ecclesia,* Lublin: Universitas Catholica, 1932.

Noval, Joseph, *Commentarium Codicis Iuris Canonici, Liber IV, De Processibus, Pars I, De Iudiciis,* Augustae Taurinorum: Marietti, 1920.

Ojetti, B., *Commentarium in Codicem Iuris Canonici, II, Lib. II, De Personis,* Romae: Universitas Gregoriana, 1928.

Onory, Sergio Mochi, *Vescovi e Citta,* Biblioteca della Rivista di Storia del Diritto Italiano, n. 8, Bologna; Zanichelli, 1933.

Ottaviani, Alaphridus, *Institutiones Iuris Publici Ecclesiastici,* 2. ed., 2 vols., Romae: Pont. Inst. Utriusque Iuris, 1935-1936.

Panormitanus, Abbas (Nicolaus de Tudeschis), *Commentaria in quinque Libros Decretalium,* 8 vols., Venetiis, 1588.

Pellegrini, Carolus, *Praxis Vicariorum,* Venetiis, 1696.

Perozzi, Silvio, *Instituzioni di Diritto Romano,* 2. ed., 2 vols., Roma: Athenaeum, 1928.

Pirhing, Ernricus, *Ius Canonicum in V Libros Decretalium,* 5 vols., Dilingae, 1674.

Poste, Edward, *Gai Institutiones or Institutes of Roman Law by Gaius,* 4. ed., revised and enlarged by E. A. Whittuck, Oxford, 1904.

Prümmer, Dominicus, *Manuale Iuris Canonici,* 4-5 ed., Friburgi Brisgoviae: Herder, 1927.

Rainer, Eligius G., *The Suspension of Clerics,* Catholic University of America Canon Law Studies, n. 111, Washington: Catholic University, 1937.

Reiffenstuel, Anacletus, *Ius Canonicum Universam,* 6 vols., Romae, 1831-1834.

Roberti, Franciscus, *De Processibus,* 2 vols., Romae: apud Aedes Facultatis Iuridicae ad S. Apollinaris, 1926.

Roffredus Beneventanus, *Tractatus in quo ordines indiciarii positiones libellique pertractantur,* Lugduni, 1561.

Rufinus, *Die Summa des Magister Rufinus,* ed. Heinrich Singer, Paderborn, 1902.

Sanchez, Thomas, *De Sancto Matrimonii Sacramento,* 3 vols., Lugduni, 1657.

Santi, Franciscus, *Praelectiones Iuris Canonici,* 2 vols., Ratisbonae, 1886.

Savigny, F., *Sistema del Diritto Romano Attuale,* translated by Vittorio Scialoja, 7 vols., Torino, 1886-1896.

Scaccia, Sigismund, *Tractatus de Appellationibus,* Coloniae, 1717.

Schmalzgrueber, Franciscus, *Ius Ecclesiasticum Universum* 6 vols. in 12, Romae, 1843-1845.

Schmier, Franciscus, *Iurisprudentia Canonico-Civilis,* 2 vols., Venetiis, 1754.

Sherman, Charles P., *Roman Law in the Modern World,* 3 ed., 3 vols., New York: Baker, Voorhis & Co., 1937.

Sipos, Stephanus, *Enchiridion Iuris Canonici,* Pecs: Haladas, 1926.

Smith, S. B., *Elements of Ecclesiastical Law, II, Ecclesiastical Trials,* New York, 1882.

——————, *The New Procedure in Criminal and Disciplinary Causes of Ecclesiastics in the United States,* 3. ed., New York, 1898.

Sohm, Rudolph, *The Institutes, a Textbook of the History and System of Roman Private Law,* translated by James C. Ledlie, 3. ed., Oxford: Clarendon Press, 1926.

Tardif, Adolphe, *Histoire des sources du droit canonique,* Paris, 1887.

Toso, Albertus, *Ad Codicem Iuris Canonici . . . Commentaria Minora,* Lib. II, tom. I, Citta di Castello: Tipografia Vinciana, 1922.

Van Hove, A., *Commentarium Lovaniense in Codicem Iuris Canonici,* Vol. I, Tom. I, *Prolegomena,* Mechliniae-Romae: H. Dessain, 1928, Vol. I, Tom. II, *De Legibus Ecclesiasticis,* Mechliniae-Romae; H. Dessain, 1929.

Vol. I, Tom. III, *De Consuetudine De Temporis Supputatione,* Mechliniae-Romae: H. Dessain, 1933.

Veranus, Cajetanus Felix, *Iuris Canonici Universi Commentarius Paratitlaris,* 5. vols., Monachii, 1703-1708.

Vermeersch, Arthur, and Creusen, J., *Epitome Iuris Canonici,* Mechliniae-Romae: H. Dessain, I, 6. ed., 1937; II-III, 5. ed., 1934-1936.

Violardo, Giacomo, *Il Pensiero Giuridico di San Girolamo*, Pubblicazioni della U. Cattolica del Sacro Guore, 2. serie, Scienze guiridiche, n. LV, Milano: Vita e Pensiero, 1937.

Vismara, Giulio, *Episcopalis Audientia*, Pubblicazioni della U. Cattolica del Sacro Cuore, 2. serie, Scienze giuridiche, n. LIV, Milano: Vita e Pensiero, 1937.

Vromant, G., *De Bonis Ecclesiae Temporalibus*, 2. ed., Louvain: Musseum Lessianum, 1934.

Wahrmund, Ludwig, *Quellen zur Geschichte des Römisch-Kanonischen Processes im Mittelalter*, Innsbruck: Verlag der Wagner' schen Universitäts-Buchhandlung, 1905—.

Wenger, Leopold, *Institutes of the Roman Law of Civil Procedure*, revised ed. translated by Otis Harrison Fisk, New York: Veritas Press, 1940.

Wernz, Franciscus Xavier, *Ius Decretalium, V, De Iudiciis Ecclesiasticis*, 3. ed., Prati, 1914.

Wernz, F. X., and Vidal, P., *Ius Canonicum, II, De Personis*, 2. ed., Romae: Universitas Gregoriana, 1928; *VI, De Processibus, ibid.*, 1927.

Woywod, Stanislaus, *A Practical Commentary on the Code of Canon Law*, 3. ed., 2 vols., New York: Herder, 1929.

Wunderlich, Agathon, *Anecdota quae Processum Civilem Spectant (Bulgarus—Damasus—Bonaguida)*, Gottingae, 1841.

Periodicals

Apollinaris, Romae, 1928—

Archiv für katholisches Kirchenrecht, Innsbruck, 1857-1861; Mainz, 1862—

Bulletino dell' Instituto di Diritto Romano, Roma, 1888—

Le Canoniste Contemporain, Paris, 1878-1926.

Il Diritto Ecclesiastico, Roma, 1896—

Ephemerides Theologicae Lovanienses, Lovanii, 1924—

The Homiletc and Pastoral Review, New York, 1900—

Jus Pontificium, Romae, 1921—

Il Monitore Ecclesiastico, Roma, 1876—

Nouvelle Revue Théologique, Paris, 1869—

Periodica de re Canonica Morali Liturgica, Bruges, 1905—

Revue historique du droit français et étranger, 4. serie, Paris, 1922—

Studia et Documenta Historiae et Iuris, Roma, 1935—

Zeitschrift der Savigny Stiftung—Kanonistische Abteilung, Weimar, 1911—

Principal Articles

Badii, Cesare, "Il dolo nel Codice di diritto canonico,"—*Il Diritto Ecclesiastico*, XL (1929), 305-326.

Besson, J., 'Sur la 'Restitution in integrum',"—*Nouvelle Revue Théologique*, XLVII (1920), 463-477.

Carelli, Edoardo, "Sul 'beneficium restitutionis',"—*Studia et Documenta Historiae et Iuris,* IV (1938), 5-67.

Crnica, A, "Defectus Codicis in designandis normis pro querela nullitatis,"—*Jus Pontificium,* XV (1935), 145-155.

D'Angelo, Sosio, "De Restitutione in Integrum iuxta canonem 1905, § 2, 4°,"—*Periodica,* XVIII (1929), 37*-62*.

————, "Un caso di 'restitutio in integrum' nella vigente disciplina canonica,"—*Ephemerides Theologicae Lovanienses,* III (1926), 355-365. (Reprinted in *Saggi su questioni guiridiche,* q. v., pp. 119-126.)

Grosso, Giuseppe, "Restitutio in Integrum,"—*Enciclopedia Italiana* (Roma, 1925-1938), XXIX, 137-138.

Hanssen, Antonius, "De Sanctione nullitatis in processu canonico,"—*Apollinaris,* XI (1938), 71-109; 215-263; 381-403; XII (1939), 198-251.

Hilling, Nikolaus, "Die fehlerhaften Rechtshandlungen und ihre Heilung,"—*AKKR,* CVII (1927), 3-32.

Oesterle, G. "De Restitutione in Integrum,"—*Jus Pontificium,* XX (1939), 174-185.

Roberti, F., "Circa limites querelae nullitatis et restitutionis in integrum,"—*Apollinaris,* I (1928), 476-483.

Romani, Silvio, [s. r]. "La Restituzione in Intero,"—*Il Monitore Ecclesiastico,* 5. series, VII (1935), 274-277.

————, "Restituzione in Intero,"—*Il Monitore Ecclesiastico,* 5. series, VII (1936), 81-84.

Solazzi, Siro, "La restitutio in integrum del pupillo,"—*Bulletino dell' Instituto di Diritto Romano,* XXVII (1914), 296-310.

Woywod, Stanislaus, "Rescissory Actions and Restitutio in Integrum,"—*Hom. Past. Rev.,* XXXI (1931), 839-846.

————, "Reinstatement in Former Position,"—*Hom. Past. Rev.,* XXXIII, part 1 (1932-1933), 375-380.

Abbreviations

AAS—Acta Apostolicae Sedis
ASS—Acta Sanctae Sedis
Bull. Rom.—Bullarium Romanum.
Bull. Rom. Cont.—Bullarii Romani Continuatio
CSEL—Corpus Scriptorum Ecclesiasticorum Latinorum
Decisiones—S. Romanae Rotae Decisiones seu Sententiae
Fontes—Codicis Iuris Canonici Fontes
h. t.—hoc titulo, always referring to *De in integrum restitutione*
Hom. Past. Rev.—The Homiletic and Pastoral Review
MGH—Monumenta Germaniae Historica
MPL—Migne, *Patrologia, Series Latina*
S. R. R.—Sacra Romana Rota
S. C. C.—Sacra Congregatio Concilii

BIOGRAPHICAL NOTE

Thomas John Feeney was born September 10, 1912, in Davenport, Iowa. There he attended Sacred Heart Cathedral School, St. Ambrose Academy, and St. Ambrose College, receiving his Bachelor of Arts degree in June, 1933. In the fall of the same year he entered the North American College, Rome, and attended theological classes at the Pontifical Gregorian University from which he received the Licentiate in Sacred Theology in July, 1937; he was ordained to the sacred priesthood on March 19, 1937, by Francesco Cardinal Marchetti-Selvaggiani, Vicar of Rome. Having returned to the Diocese of Davenport, he taught English for one year at St. Ambrose College. He was enrolled in the School of Canon Law at the Catholic University of America in the fall of 1938 and received the Baccalaureate in Canon Law in June, 1939, the Licentiate in Canon Law in June, 1940.

ALPHABETICAL INDEX

Absence, 9, 30, 63
Adults, 9-10, 30, 61-68, 101-102
Age of majority, 9, 29, 55-56
Alexander III, decretal of, 22-25
Alienation of church property, 23, 71-72
Appeal, 96-101
  prohibited, 97-101
  restoration to, 143-145
  time allowed for, 96
Appellatione remota, 31, 97
Arbiters, 35, 83-84
Arbitrators, 83-84
Audientia episcopalis, 13-14

Benedict XIV, 40-42, 119
Benedict XV, chirograph of, 47, 124
Bernard of Pavia, 24-25

Cause, righteous, for *restitutio,* 54
  absence, 9, 30, 63
  error, 11, 65-67
  fear, 10, 63-65
  ignorance, 65-67
  minority, 9, 29, 55-58
  others, 10, 67
Citation,
  restitutio against, 76
  in case of *restitutio,* 87
Civil law,
  on age, 29, 55
  on prescription, 74-75
  on contracts, 69, 72, 74
  on *restitutio,* 72, 74-75
Confession, judicial, 75-76
Contempt of court, 125
  appeal of one in, 98-100
Continuous time, 79-82, 102
Contracts, 30, 56, 71-74
Court, competent, 131-135
Damage, grave, 7, 28, 51-52
D'Angelo, opinion of, 117 ff.

Defender of the bond, 95-96, 114, 118
Definition, 1-2, 49 ff
Delegated judges, 35-36, 83, 132
Documents,
  false, 107-109
  new, 105-107
Donation, 75

Effects of *restitutio,*
  against the sentence, 37-38, 137-140
  in general, 37-38, 90-93
Emancipation of minors, 9, 57-58
Equity, 1, 52, 56
Error, 11, 65-67
Execution of sentence, 137-138
Extraordinary remedy, 51

Fatalia, 78, 143-145
Fear, 10, 63-65
Footnotes of Code, 119, 126
Force, 10, 65
Fraud, 11, 65
  of one party, 109-110, 133
Fruits, restoration of, 91-92

Gratian, Decree of, 19-21

Heirs of minors, 58, 60

Imputability of damage, 10, 62, 102
Ignorance, 65-67
  presumption of, 66
Injustice of *res iudicata,* 104 ff, 111 ff, 115, 122-123, 129
Isidore of Seville, 15
Ives of Chartres, 18-19

Jerome, St., 15
Judge, competent, 82-85, 131-134
Leo I, 14
Libellus, introductory, 36, 87

Mandate, procurator's, 37, 87-88, 136
Marriage, 70
  cases concerning, 41-44, 95-96
Minors, 9-10, 29, 55-58, 101-103
Moral persons, 29-30, 58-60

Neglect of law, 111 ff, 133-134, 136
Nullity of sentence, 32-33, 100-101, 114-120, 124-130
Nullity of acts, 69

Oath, decisory, 109-110
Object of *restitutio*,
  contracts, 30, 71-74
  extra-judicial matters, 31, 70-75
  judicial matters, 31, 75-78
  sentence, 12, 31-33, 94 ff
Officialis, 83

Perjury, 109-110
Plaint of nullity, 114-116, 118, 120, 122, 124-127, 129-130
  for irremediable nullity, 100
  for remediable nullity, 100-101
Prescription, 30-31, 74-75, 79
Privilege, 50
Procurator,
  need of mandate, 37, 87-88, 136
  fraud of, 110
Profession, religious, 39-41, 70, 95
Promoter of justice, 85-86, 88-89, 114, 118, 125, 127, 136

Querela nullitatis, cf, plaint of nullity

Regolamento of Gregory XVI, 45-46, 117, 119
Renuntiation of appeal, 100
Rescissory actions, 50, 70
Res iudicata, 95-96
Res mixti fori, 70-71
Restitutio in integrum,
  decretal law, 22 ff
    conditions, 27
    effects, 37
    object, 30
    procedure, 35
    subject, 29
    time limit, 34
  present law against the sentence,
    conditions, 94
    effects, 137
    procedure, 135
  present law, in general,
    causes, 54
    effects, 90
    procedure, 85
    subject, 54 ff.
    time limit, 79
  Roman law, 5 ff
    causes, 8-11
    conditions, 7
    procedure, 11-12
    time limit, 8
Roberti, opinion of, 114 ff
Roman law, 5-12
Rota, S. R., 44-45
  chief cases cited, 126-128, 134
  competence of, 84, 134
  Madrid Rota, 134
  Regulae of, 46

Sale, contract of, 74, 90
Schemata of the Code, 50, 58, 120, 125-126
Sentence,
  restitutio against, 94 ff
  criminal, 140-143
  interlocutory, 98
Signatura, Apostolic, 45-47
  chief cases cited, 124-125
  competence of, 84, 133, 135
  Regulae of, 46-47, 117, 119-120
Subject of *restitutio*,
  adults, 9-11, 30, 61-68, 101-102
  minors, 9, 29, 55-58, 101-103
  moral persons, 29-30, 58-60
Subornation of witnesses, 110

Trent, Council of, 39-40
Tribunal,
  competent 131-135
  illegitimately constituted, 100

Usable time, 79-80, 102, 136

Witnesses,
  in lieu of documents, 106-108
  perjured, 106
  subornation of, 110
  unsworn, 137

CANON LAW STUDIES

1. Freriks, Rev. Celestine A., C.PP.S., J.C.D., Religious Congregations in Their External Relations, 121 pp., 1916.
2. Galliher, Rev. Daniel M., O.P., J.C.D., Canonical Elections, 117 pp., 1917.
3. Borkowski, Rev. Aurelius L., O.F.M., J.C.D., De Confraternitatibus Ecclesiasticis, 136 pp., 1918.
4. Castillo, Rev. Cayo, J.C.D., Disertacion Historico-Canonica sobre la Potestad del Cabildo en Sede Vacante o Impedida del Vicario Capitular, 99 pp., 1919 (1918).
5. Kubelbeck, Rev. William J., S.T.B., J.C.D., The Sacred Pentitentiaria and Its Relations to Faculties of Ordinaries and Priests, 129 pp., 1918.
6. Petrovits, Rev. Joseph J.C., S.T.D., J.C.D., The New Church Law On Matrimony, X-461 pp., 1919.
7. Hickey, Rev. John J., S.T.B., J.C.D., Irregularities and Simple Impediments in the New Code of Canon Law, 100 pp., 120.
8. Klekotka, Rev. Peter J., S.T.B., J.C.D., Diocesan Consultors, 179 pp., 1920.
9. Wanenmacher, Rev. Francis, J.C.D., The Evidence in Ecclesiastical Procedure Affecting the Marriage Bond, 1920 (Printed 1935).
10. Golden, Rev. Henry Francis, J.C.D., Parochial Benefices in the New Code, IV-119 pp., 1921 (Printed 1925).
11. Koudelka, Rev. Charles J., J.C.D., Pastors, Their Rights and Duties According to the New Code of Canon Law, 211 pp., 1921.
12. Melo, Rev. Antonius, O.F.M., J.C.D., De Exemptione Regularium, X-188 pp., 1921.
13. Schaaf, Rev. Valentine Theodore, O.F.M., S.T.B., J.C.D., The Cloister, X-180 pp., 1921.
14. Burke, Rev. Thomas Joseph, S.T.D., J.C.D., Competence in Ecclesiastical Tribunals, IV-117 pp., 1922.
15. Leech, Rev. George Leo, J.C.D., A Comparative Study of the Constitution, "Apostolicae Sedis" and the "Codex Juris Canonici," 179 pp., 1922.
16. Motry, Rev. Hubert Louis, S.T.D., J.C.D., Diocesan Faculties According to the Code of Canon Law, II-167 pp., 1922.
17. Murphy, Rev. George Lawrence, J.C.D., Delinquencies and Penalties in the Administration and Reception of the Sacraments, IV-121 pp., 1923.
18. O'Reilly, Rev. John Anthony, S.T.B., J.C.D., Ecclesiastical Sepulture in the New Code of Canon Law, II-129 pp., 1923.

19. Michalicka, Rev. Wenceslas Cyrill, O.S.B., J.C.D., Judicial Procedure in Dismissal of Clerical Exempt Religious, 107 pp., 1923.
20. Dargin, Rev. Edward Vincent, S.T.B., J.C.D., Reserved Cases According to the Code of Canon Law, IV-103, pp., 1924.
21. Godfrey, Rev. John A., S.T.B., J.C.D., The Right of Patronage According to the Code of Canon Law, 153 pp., 1924.
22. Hagedorn, Rev. Francis Edward, J.C.D., General Legislation on Indulgences, II-154 pp., 1924.
23. King, Rev. James Ignatius, J.C.D., The Administration of the Sacraments to Dying Non-Catholics, V-141 pp., 1924.
24. Winslow, Rev. Francis Joseph, A.F.M., J.C.D., Vicars and Prefects Apostolic, IV-149 pp., 1924.
25. Correa, Rev. Jose Servelion, S.T.L., J.C.D., La Potestad Legislativa de la Iglesia Catolica, IV-127 pp., 1925.
26. Dugan, Rev. Henry Francis, A.M., J.C.D., The Judiciary Department of the Diocesan Curia, 87 pp., 1925.
27. Keller, Rev. Charles Frederick, S.T.B., J.C.D., Mass Stipends, 167 pp., 1925.
28. Paschang, Rev. John Linus, J.C.D., The Sacramentals According to the Code of Canon Law, 129 pp., 1925.
29. Pointek, Rev. Cyrillus, O.F.M., S.T.B., J.C.D., De Indulto Exclaustrationis necnon Saecularizationis, XIII-289 pp., 1925.
30. Kearney, Rev. Richard Joseph, S.T.B., J.C.D., Sponsors at Baptism According to the Code of Canon Law, IV-127 pp., 1925.
31. Bartlett, Rev. Chester Joseph, A.M., LL.B., J.C.D., The Tenure of Parochial Property in the United States of America, V-108 pp., 1926.
32. Kilker, Rev. Adrian Jerome, J.C.D., Extreme Unction, V-425 pp., 1926.
33. McCormick, Rev. Robert Emmett, J.C.D., Confessors of Religious, VIII-266 pp., 1926.
34. Miller, Rev. Newton Thomas. J.C.D., Founded Masses According to the Code of Canon Law, VII-93 pp., 1926.
35. Roelker, Rev. Edward G., S.T.D., J.C.D., Principles of Privilege According to the Code of Canon Law, XI-166 pp., 1926.
36. Bakalarczyk, Rev. Richardus, M.I.C., J.U.D., De Novitiatu, VIII-208 pp., 1927.
37. Pizzuti, Rev. Lawrence, O.F.M., J.U.L., De Parochis Religiosis, 1927. (Not printed).
38. Bliley, Rev. Nicholas Martin, O.S.B., J.C.D., Altars According to the Code of Canon Law, XIX-132 pp., 1927.
39. Brown, Mr. Brendan Francis, A.B. LL.M., J.U.D., The Canonical Juristic Personality with Special Reference to Its Status in the United States of America, V-212 pp., 1927.

40. Cavanaugh, Rev. William Thomas, C.P., J.U.D., The Reservation of the Blessed Sacrament, VIII-101 pp., 1927.
41. Doheny, Rev. William J., C.S.C., A.B., J.U.D., Church Property: Modes of Acquisition, X-118 pp., 1927.
42. Feldhaus, Rev. Aloysius H., C.PP.S., J.C.D., Oratories, IX-141 pp., 1927.
43. Kelly, Rev. James Patrick, A.B., J.C.D., The Jurisdiction of the Simple Confessor, X-208 pp., 1927.
44. Neuberger, Rev. Nicholas J., J.C.D., Canon 6 or the Relation of the Codex Juris Canonici to the Preceding Legislation, V-95 pp., 1927.
45. O'Keefe, Rev. Gerald Michael, J.C.D., Matrimonial Dispensations, Powers of Bishops, Priests and Confessors, VIII-232 pp., 1927.
46. Quigley, Rev. Joseph A.M., A.B., J.C.B., Condemned Societies, 139 pp., 1927.
47. Zaplotnik, Rev. Johannes Leo, J.C.D., De Vicariis Foraneis, X-142 pp., 1927.
48. Duskie, Rev. John Aloysius, A.B., J.C.D., The Canonical Status of the Orientals in the United States, VIII-196 pp., 1928.
49. Hyland, Rev. Francis Edward, J.C.D., Excommunication, Its Nature, Historical Development and Effects, VIII-181 pp., 1928.
50. Reinmann, Rev. Gerald Joseph, O.M.C., J.C.D., The Third Order Secular of Saint Francis, 201 pp., 1928.
51. Schenk, Rev. Francis J., J.C.D., The Matrimonial Impediments of Mixed Religion and Disparity of Cult, XVI-318 pp., 1929.
52. Coady, Rev. John Joseph, S.T.D., J.U.D., A.M., The Appointment of Pastors, VIII-150 pp., 1929.
53. Kay, Rev. Thomas Henry, J.C.D., Competence in Matrimonial Procedure, VIII-164 pp., 1929.
54. Turner, Rev. Sidney Joseph, C.P., J.U.D., The Vow of Poverty, XLIX-217 pp., 1929.
55. Kearney, Rev. Raymond, A., A.B., S.T.D., J.C.D., The Principles, of Delegation, VII-149 pp., 1929.
56. Conran, Rev. Edward James, A.B., J.C.D., The Interdict, V-163 pp., 1930.
57. O'Neil, Rev. William H., J.C.D., Papal Rescripts of Favor, VII-218 pp., 1930.
58. Bastnagel, Rev. Clement Vincent, J.U.D., The Appointment of Parochial Adjutants and Assistants, XV-257 pp., 1930.
59. Ferry, Rev. William A., A.B., J.C.D., Stole Fees, V-135 pp., 1930.
60. Costello, Rev. John Michael, A.B., J.C.D., Domicile and Quasi-domicile, VII-201 pp., 1930.
61. Kremer, Rev. Michael Nicholas, A.B., S.T.B., J.C.D., Church Support in the United States, VI-1930.

62. Angulo, Rev. Luis, C.M., J.C.D., Legislation de la Iglesia sobre la intencion en la application de la Santa Misa, VII-104 pp., 1931.
63. Frey, Rev. Wolfgang Norbert, O.S.B., A.B., J.C.D., The Act of Religious Profession, VIII-174 pp., 1931.
64. Roberts, Rev. James Brendan, A.B., J.C.D., The Banns of Marriage, XIV-140 pp., 1931.
65. Ryder, Rev. Raymond Aloysius, A.B., J.C.D., Simony, IX-151 pp., 1931.
66. Campagna, Rev. Angelo, Ph.D., J.U.D., Il Vicario Generale del Vescovo, VII-205 pp., 1931.
67. Cox, Rev. Joseph Godfrey, A.B., J.C.D., The Administration ot Seminaries, VI-124 pp., 1931.
68. Gregory, Rev. Donald J., J.U.D., The Pauline Privilege, XV-165 pp., 1931.
69. Donohue, Rev. John F., J.C.D., The Impediment of Crime, VII-110 pp., 1931.
70. Dooley, Rev. Eugene A., O.M.I., J.C.D., Church Law On Sacred Relics, IX-143 pp., 1931.
71. Orth, Rev. Raymond Clement, O.M.C., J.C.D., The Approbation of Religious Institutes, 171 pp., 1931.
72. Pernicone, Rev. Joseph M., A.B., J.C.D., The Ecclesiastical Prohibition of Books, XII-267 pp., 1932.
73. Clinton, Rev. Connell, A.B., J.C.D., The Paschal Precept, IX-108 pp., 1932.
74. Donnelly, Rev. Francis B., A.M., S.T.L., J.C.D., The Diocesan Synod, VIII-125 pp., 1932.
75. Torrente, Rev. Camilo, C.M.F., J.C.D., Las Processiones Sagradas, V-145 pp., 1932.
76. Murphy, Rev. Edwin J., C.PP.S., J.C.D., Suspension Ex Informata Conscientia, XI-122, pp., 1932.
77. Mackenzie, Rev. Eric F., A.M., S.T.L., J.C.D., The Delict of Heresy in its Commission Penalization, Absolution, VII-124 pp., 1932.
78. Lyons Rev. Avitus E., S.T.B., J.C.D., The Collegiate Tribunal of First Instance, XI-147 pp., 1932.
79. Connolly, Rev. Thomas A., J.C.D., Appeals, XI-195 pp., 1932.
80. Sangmeister, Rev. Joseph V., A.B., J.C.D., Force and Fear as Precluding Matrimonial Consent, V-211 pp., 1932.
81. Jaeger, Rev. Leo A., A.B., J.C.D., The Administration of Vacant and Quasi-vacant Episcopal Sees in the United States, IX-229 pp., 1932.
82. Rimlinger, Rev. Herbert T., J.C.D., Error Invalidating Matrimonial Consent, VII-79 pp., 1932.
83. Barrett, Rev. John D.M., S.S., J.C.D., A Comparative Study of the Third Plenary Council of Baltimore and the Code, IX-221 pp., 1932.

84. Carberry, Rev. John J., Ph.D., S.T.D., J.C.D., The Juridical Form of Marriage, X-177 pp., 1934.
85. Dolan, Rev. John L., A.B., J.C.D., The Defensor Vinculi, XII-157 pp., 1934.
86. Hannan, Rev. Jerome D., A.M., S.T.D., LL.B., J.C.D., The Canon Law of Wills, IX-517 pp., 1934.
87. Lemieux, Rev. Delisle A., A.M., J.C.D., The Sentence in Ecclesiastical Procedure, IX-131 pp., 1934.
88. O'Rourke, Rev. James J., A.B., J.C.D., Parish Registers, VII-109 pp., 1934.
89. Timlin, Rev. Bartholomew, O.F.M., A.M., J.C.D., Conditional Matrimonial Consent, X-381 pp., 1934.
90. Wahl, Rev. Francis X., A.B., J.C.D., The Matrimonial Impediments of Consanguinity and Affinity, VI-125 pp., 1934.
91. White, Rev. Robert J., A.B., LL.B., S.T.B., J.C.D., Canonical Ante-Nuptial Promises and the Civil Law, VI-152 pp., 1934.
92. Herrera, Rev. Antonio Parra, O.C.D., J.C.D., Legislation Ecclesiastica sobra el Ayuno y la Abstinencia, XI-191 pp., 1935.
93. Kennedy, Rev. Edwin J., J.C.D., The Special Matrimonial Process in Cases of Evident Nullity, X-165 pp., 1935.
94. Manning, Rev. John J., A.B., J.C.D., Presumption of Law in Matrimonial Procedure, XI-111 pp., 1935.
95. Moeder, Rev. John M., J.C.D., The Proper Bishop for Ordination and Dismissorial Letters, VII-135 pp., 1935.
96. O'Mara, Rev. William A., A.B., J.C.D., Canonical Causes For Matrimonial Dispensations, IX-155 pp., 1935.
97. Reilly, Rev. Peter, J.C.D., Residence of Pastors, IX-81 pp., 1935.
98. Smith, Rev. Mariner T., O.P., S.T.L., J.C.D., The Penal Law For Religious, VII-169 pp., 1935.
99. Whalen, Rev. Donald W., A.M., J.C.D., The Value of Testimonial Evidence in Matrimonial Procedure, XIII-297 pp., 1935.
100. Cleary, Rev. Joseph F., J.C.D., Canonical Limitations on the Alienation of Church Property, VIII-141 pp., 1936.
101. Glynn, Rev. John C., J.C.D., The Promoter of Justice, XX-337 pp., 1936.
102. Brennan, Rev. James H., S.S., A.M., S.T.B., J.C.D., The Simple Convalidation of Marriage, VI-135 pp, 1937.
103. Brunini, Rev. Joseph Bernard, J.C.D., The Clerical Obligations of Canons, 139 and 142, X-121 pp., 1937.
104. Connor, Rev. Maurice, A.B., J.C.D., The Administrative Removal of Pastors, VIII-159 pp., 1937.
105. Guilfoyle, Rev. Merlin Joseph, J.C.D., Custom, XI-144 pp., 1937.
106. Hughes, Rev. James Austin, A.B., A.M., J.C.D., Witnesses in Criminal Trials of Clerics, IX-140 pp., 1937.

107. Jansen, Rev. Raymond J., A.B., S.T.L., J.C.D., Canonical Provisions for Catechetical Instruction, VII-153 pp., 1937.
108. Kealy, Rev. John James, A.B., J.C.D,, The Introductory Libellus in Church Court Procedure, XI-121 pp., 1937.
109. McManus, Rev. James Edward, C.SS.R., J.C.D., The Administration of Temporal Goods in Religious Institutes, XVI-196 pp., 1937.
110. Moriarity, Rev. Eugene James, J.C.D., Oaths in Ecclesiastical Courts, X-115 pp., 1937.
111. Rainer, Rev. Eligius George, C.SS.R., J.C.D., Suspension of Clerics, XVII-249 pp., 1937.
112. Reilly, Rev. Thomas F., C.SS.R., J.C.D., Visitation of Religious, VI-195 pp., 1938.
113. Moriarty, Rev. Francis E., C.SS.R., J.C.D., The Extraordinary Absolution from Censures, XV-334 pp., 1938.
114. Connolly, Rev. Nicholas P., J.C.D., The Canonical Erection of Parishes, X-132 pp., 1938.
115. Donovan, Rev. James Joseph, J.C.D., The Pastor's Obligation in Prenuptial Investigation, XII-322 pp., 1938.
116. Harrigan, Rev. Robert J., M.A., S.T.B., J.C.D., The Radical Sanation of Invalid Marriages, VIII-208 pp., 1938.
117. Boffa, Rev. Conrad Humbert, J.C.D., Canonical Provisions for Catholic Schools, X-211 pp., 1939.
118. Parsons, Rev. Anscar John, O.M. Cap., J.C.D., Canonical Elections, XII-236 pp., 1939.
119. Reilly, Rev. Edward Michael, A.B., J.C.D., The General Norms of Dispensation, X-156 pp., 1939.
120. Ryan, Rev. Gerald Aloysius, A.B., J.C.D., Principles of Episcopal Jurisdiction, XII-172 pp., 1939.
121. Burton, Rev. Francis James, C.S.C., A.B., J.C.D., A Commentary on Canon 1125, X-222 pp., 1940.
122. Miaskiewicz, Rev. Francis Sigismund, J.C.D., Supplied Jurisdiction according to Canon 209, XII-340 pp., 1940.
123. Rice, Rev. Patrick William, A.B., J.C.D., Proof of Death in Prenuptial Investigation, VIII-156 pp., 1940.
124. Anglin, Rev. Thomas Francis, M.S., J.C.L., The Eucharistic Fast.
125. Coleman, Rev. John Jerome, J.C.L., The Minister of Confirmation.
126. Downs, Rev. John Emmanuel, A.B., J.C.L., The Concept of Clerical Immunity.
127. Esswein, Rev. Anthony Albert, J.C.L., Extrajudicial Penal Powers of Ecclesiastical Superiors.
128. Farrell, Rev. Benjamin Francis, M.A., S.T.L., J.C.L., The Rights and Duties of the Local Ordinary Regarding Congregations of Women Religious of Pontifical Approval.

129. Feeney, Rev. Thomas John, A.B., S.T.L., J.C.L., Restitutio in Integrum.
130. Findlay, Rev. Stephen William, O.S.B., A.B., J.C.L., Canonical Norms Governing the Deposition and Degradation of Clerics.
131. Goodwine, Rev. John, A.B., S.T.L., J.C.L., The Right of the Church to Acquire Property.
132. Heston, Rev. Edward Louis, C.S.C., Ph.D., S.T.D., J.C.L., The Alienation of Church Property in the United States .
133. Hogan, Rev. James John, S.T.L., J.C.L.,, Judicial Advocates and Procurators.
134. Kealy, Rev. Thomas M., A.B., Litt. B., J.C.L., Dowry of Women Religious.
135. Keene, Rev. Michael James, O.S.B., J.C.L., Religious Ordinaries and Canon 198.
136. Kerin, Rev. Charles A., S.S., M.A., S.T.B., J.C.L., The Privation of Christian Burial.
137. Louis, Rev. William Francis, M.A., J.C.L., Diocesan Archives.
138. McDevitt, Rev. Gilbert Joseph, A.B., J.C.L., Legitimacy and Legitimation.
139. McDonough, Rev. Thomas Joseph, A.B., J.C.L., Apostolic Administrators.
140. Meier, Rev. Carl Anthony, A.B., J.C.L., Penal Administrative Procedure Against Negligent Pastors.
141. Schmidt, Rev. John Rogg, A.B., J.C.L., The Principles of Authentic Interpretation in Canon 17 of the Code of Canon Law.
142. Slafkosky, Rev. Andrew Leonard, A.B., J.C.L., The Canonical Episcopal Visitation of the Diocese.
143. Swoboda, Rev. Innocent Robert, O.F.M., J.C.L., Ignorance in Relation to the Imputability of Delicts.
144. Dubé, Rev. Arthur Joseph, A.B., J.C.L., The General Principles for the Reckoning of Time in Canon Law.
145. McBride, Rev. James T., A.B., J.C.L., Incardination and Excardination of Seculars.

www.ingramcontent.com/pod-product-compliance
Lightning Source LLC
LaVergne TN
LVHW050229080826
844660LV00012B/498

* 9 7 8 0 8 1 3 2 2 3 1 8 6 *